Retooling the Church

FINDING YOUR PLACE IN MINISTRY

Doug,
I'm so thankful for the friendship we have developed. Friends like you help me to think higher and believe for more. Thanks

Ken

Retooling the Church

FINDING YOUR PLACE IN MINISTRY

RON SATRAPE

DESTINY IMAGE® PUBLISHERS, INC.

P.O. Box 310, Shippensburg, PA 17257-0310

"Speaking to the Purposes of God for this Generation and for the Generations to Come."

This book and all other Destiny Image, Revival Press, Mercy Place, Fresh Bread, Destiny Image Fiction, and Treasure House books are available at Christian bookstores and distributors worldwide.

For a U.S. bookstore nearest you, call **1-800-722-6774**.
For more information on foreign distributors, call **717-532-3040**.
Or reach us on the Internet: **www.destinyimage.com**

ISBN 10: 0-7684-2438-0
ISBN 13: 978-0-7684-2438-6

For Worldwide Distribution, Printed in the U.S.A.

1 2 3 4 5 6 7 8 9 10 11 / 09 08 07 06

CONTENTS

FOREWORD

There is a new paradigm shift in Christian leadership taking place now in the Body of Christ. The Holy Spirit is moving His leadership from a "top-down" model to a team model. When Jesus first introduced His ministry, He came in functioning as a top-down leader but before He left He transitioned to a leadership team.

Jesus knew that ministry could not go forward if it was focused on the security of His own ministry. He knew that the building up of the Kingdom must be centered on others. Jesus reproduced Himself in the Twelve who then reproduced themselves in others and the reproduction process began. Thus the Church—the Body of Christ and the Army of God— was released to take the gospel to the nations.

Ron Satrape has hit a home run with his book *Retooling the Church.* Leaders must embrace this revelation and make the necessary changes needed to lead our congregations into this new wineskin. If you are searching for answers to what the Holy Spirit is saying to the Church then I believe this book can give you direction and answer many of your questions. Ron not only teaches but has walked it out. His life is a living testimony that it works.

Terry Nance
Author, *God's Armor Bearer*

PREFACE

This book is a result of more than 25 years of pastoral ministry and the passion to move today's Church into fulfilling the needs of modern-day believers. Although I address charismatic church leaders specifically, the team and leadership concepts apply to Christians involved in a wide variety of situations and organizational structures. Based on a solid biblical foundation, the lessons shared have the power to enhance and improve the inner workings of your church, business, ministry, career, and life.

CHAPTER 1

RETOOLING THE LEADERSHIP MODEL

I started in the ministry during the charismatic movement in the early 1970s. At that time the Holy Spirit was virtually unknown in the typical denominational churches. The Church had become so structured and planned that God had no room to move. For the most part, the gifts of the Holy Spirit were not being used and were not welcomed in the formal and traditional church setting of the day. Local church theology was not receptive to charismatic theology or allowing the gifts of the Holy Spirit to operate during worship services.

Consequently, the Full Gospel Businessman's Fellowship membership increased during those years because people hungered to experience God in a personal and real way. There was a need for a paradigm change in the way denominational churches were structured and the charismatic churches began to fill that need.

The Holy Spirit raised up a new breed of top-down leaders who pioneered a new Spirit-filled move of God. A prophetic leader led us into this new move of God. How we "did church" changed and the top-down leadership model was the way to assure that we wouldn't be voted or politicked out of what the Holy Spirit was doing in this new movement.

Jesus Christ operated in the top-down prophetic leader mode when He began His ministry. At that time, the religious system had become corrupted and had strayed from rightly reflecting the character and nature of God. God came in person to retool His Church. The Son of God said, "No!" to what was happening within His Body. His ministry began as He modeled His Father: "This is what I'm like. When you see Me, you see the Father."

Top-down leadership is most valuable in the start-up stage of ministry. We need top-down guidance from the prophetic leader who points us in a new direction—back to God and God's ways. Jesus forever changed religion as they knew it during His day. He led that change as a top-down leader. He made all the calls. He told His disciples what to do and they did it. This type of leadership model is seen throughout the Scriptures—Noah, Abraham, Isaac, Jacob, and Moses all brought great change and renewed direction to God's people as top-down, entrepreneurial, pioneering leaders.

MOVING BEYOND TOP-DOWN

The modern-day charismatic church was launched with a top-down leadership structure. But what was good for the beginning may be the very thing that stands in the way of expanding and developing the future charismatic church. I believe we need to move beyond our beginnings if the Church is to experience continued growth—or even continued existence.

Over time, one weakness of the top-down leadership model became evident: lack of "buy in." Followers of the top-down leader do not always fully embrace the faith, character, and lifestyle of their leader as their own. Because of that weakness, today's typical charismatic Christian reflects very little of the values and character of their top-down leader. I believe that we are facing a crisis concerning American charismatic Christians living out the biblical values and ideals being preached and taught in the pulpits across the country.

Unfortunately, many vary little from the unchurched regarding character and values. Christians divorce, are addicted, and struggle with the same ills as our lost neighbors. Many Christians don't value morality, honesty, or integrity any more than the unchurched do. Many Christians allow their top-down leaders to live out Christianity for them—living vicariously through them. The standard is different for the pulpit than it is for the pew.

TEAM-UP LEADERSHIP

I'm so thankful for the insight of Patrick Lencioni, who authored the book *The Five Dysfunctions of a Team*[1]. Reading that book changed my life and ministry forever because I recognized some of the long-term weaknesses of the top-down leadership model we had learned in the church. I also recognized the even greater weaknesses that resulted from the democratic- or consensus-driven leadership models.

My father was a Southern Baptist pastor who had planted several churches that were all congregationally ruled. In my experience, democracy in churches creates politics instead of spiritual leadership. Rick Warren, the Southern Baptist pastor of Saddleback Church in Lake Forest, California, developed a cutting-edge team model that works better without democracy. As far as I know, the only democratic thing that Saddleback Church does is allow the congregation to vote on the annual budget that's submitted by their pastoral team.

Team-up leadership is successful in the church and business environment. It is not without drawbacks, though—drawbacks that, if recognized, can be overcome. Patrick Lencioni is the first business leader I read that defines a model of leadership that falls between the extremes of top-down and consensus-driven. His secular book greatly influenced our ministry team model, and I believe is a must-read for every leader.

The remainder of the book is devoted to developing and strengthening your church, ministry, or outreach by using all the resources God gave you—the people involved in your work. Retooling the Church with a team-up leadership model empowers everyone to become who God intended them to be.

ENDNOTE

1. Patrick M. Lencioni, *The Five Dysfunctions of a Team: A Leadership Fable* (San Francisco: Jossey-Bass, 2002).

CHAPTER 2

RECOGNIZING THE "NO TEAM" SYMPTOMS

WHY MOST CHRISTIANS DON'T "BUY INTO" CHURCH

Have you ever wondered why only 20 percent of the people in the church really buy into it? It's been my experience that the 20 percent who buy in are the ones who do 80 percent of the giving and serving. The 80 percent who *don't* buy in contribute the remaining 20 percent of what needs to be given and done.

Maybe you're thinking "not in my church." Maybe your church, like ours, got up to 50 or 60 percent of the people attending, tithing, and serving. That's better, but 100 percent buy-in should be our goal.

Unfortunately, many Christians think of church like a restaurant. They arrive, they are served, and they go home. They are being fed but not being changed. They're not being changed because they aren't buying into the truth that they are being fed. The communication is one way—from the pulpit to the pew. The leadership structure is also one way—from the top down to the bottom.

Many Christians are consumers who walk the aisles of options and take a little of this truth and a little of that. They concoct their own religion that is often a mixture of "success in life," reincarnation, and whatever Bible promises match up with their needs in life at that particular time. They change the television channels at home or at the churches they attend until they find something that satisfies their current needs. Here again, the television provides only one-way communication—from the evangelist to the viewer.

Before long they realize that their self-concocted faith isn't working and they move on to something or someone else. As consumers, they wander from one supermarket (church) to another, never really buying into a faith that they would give their life to defend.

TRUTH TRANSFORMS

People have truth exposure—not truth transformation. People are exposed to the truth, but not affected by it. It is information that they know, but it does not become a part of who they are. There is no inward formation. It simply does not play out in their lifestyle.

Transformation takes place when the hearer is enrolled into a discipleship process with an influential leader. The influential leader helps the hearer buy into the truth. Solid faith is the result of buying into the truth—hook, line, sinker, fishing pole, fisherman, and dock.

In my 25 years of pastoral experience, the truth is that *our needs* instead of *our God* have become the center of our faith. Too many times Christians think that God exists for the sole purpose of blessing and meeting needs. This kind of self-serving, self-centered faith is unfulfilling and empty. We need a cause to sacrifice for and invest in. We need a Bible faith—one we will defend and die for.

Bible faith caused Abram to leave his comforts and country and follow a God who promised to transform him and make a nation out of him. Bible faith led three young men to choose a fiery furnace rather than deny their God. Bible faith caused Moses to reject a royal lifestyle and become a slave.

This faith, the faith of our Hebrew and Christian fathers, caused thousands to choose martyrdom rather than deny or disobey their God.

TOO COMFORTABLE

Why don't people buy into the faith and the Church today? Because we've told them they don't have to. Our co-dependent American culture has convinced us that someone else will pay for it, be responsible, do it, teach it, learn it, earn it, etc. Believers see the need for prosperity and success but are blind to the need for character and transformation. We aren't sold on the damage our sin and wickedness does to the ones we love and ourselves. We have had our own way so long that we don't know what it's like to be without our way.

Unfortunately, too many Christians are ignorant to the effect our immaturity has on real prosperity and significant blessing. We haven't bought into our need to be Christ-like or realized the impact our life and lifestyles have on unbelievers. In this day of megachurches, many church leaders' self-image is determined by how big the Sunday morning crowd is or how large the bank account has grown. We belong to the "first church" so we think we are better than others. Today's measurement of progress in life is having and having more.

We haven't bought into the faith of the Bible that measures progress in character and Christ-likeness. We haven't bought into "godliness with contentment being great gain." Many Christians' selfish faith hasn't provided what it promised, and they have quit buying it.

Could it be that church leaders have painted themselves into a corner? Have we given people what they thought they wanted and now they're not buying it because they realize that they need more?

LEADERSHIP—THE GREATEST NEED

The greatest Church need of the hour is leadership. There is a dearth of leadership in the Church resulting in the decline of Christian character and in new convert-driven church growth. We must change how we lead others to follow Christ. Our faith must become theirs. We need to retool the Church through a new model or pattern that other leaders and followers buy into.

The United States is the only country in the world that is decreasing in numeric church growth. Christianity is growing in numbers everywhere except in our country.[1] That may surprise you; but according to church pollster and researcher, George Barna, not only are we declining, but we're seeing a parallel moral decline in those who say they're Christians. For example, a 2004 Barna Group study revealed that Christians divorce at the same rate as non-Christians.[2] Christians are almost as addicted as the rest of our society. We have very similar moral standards.[3] Unfortunately, it seems as if there is very little difference in our country between the churched and the unchurched.

As a pastor, I noticed this trend some years ago and became so discouraged that I almost quit the ministry. I almost became one of the 70 percent of Protestant ministers who quit the ministry before they are 50 years old. At that time, I had a leader who had come up under our ministry. We had invested years into the person's development. Sadly, this person became disgruntled and offended and left—along with about 70 people from our congregation. I couldn't understand how someone could do that, and it caused me to re-examine our ministry. I knew in my heart that something was not right within the ministry.

As I considered the congregation, I realized how little the people had changed over the years. Some couples were getting divorced. Many of the regular folks were still struggling with anger, depression, addictions, pornography—you name it and it was still with us. I took a long hard look at our church body and I had to admit something was missing. I realized that people weren't changing or if they were changing, it was at a snail's pace.

Then the worst, and best, thing happened. I followed the problem—all the way back to me. How much was I changing? Although I didn't have any of the aforementioned problems, I couldn't see much recent improvement and growth in my own life. I decided to set out on a mission to find out what was missing in the church. I asked around: "Can anyone tell me what's missing in this church?" No one gave me an answer. As a last resort, I sought the Lord about the issue. One day He revealed to me what was drastically missing in our church. It rang out like a liberty bell—*Jesus Christ is missing!*

When Jesus Christ is absent from church, He is absent from us. People can't see Him in us. We were having church. We hosted events and people were getting saved, healed, and delivered, but there was little change in them. We had no real process for transformation. As a result, people weren't buying into our beliefs and values for any significant amount of time. We were *exposing* people to the truth but not *leading them through* transformation.

Leadership is not a position—it is the influence leaders wield. As a leader, my impact is felt more by my *influence* than by my *position.* Leadership is most effectively expressed to others when we become life coaches and mentors, instead of rulers and governors. In my particular experience in our church, we were feeding people but we weren't influencing them to follow and buy into the truths and lifestyle of Jesus Christ.

The greatest need of the hour is t*o lead others to follow Christ*—not just feed on Him. People feed but they will not follow. It takes leadership not ruler-ship to influence people to follow leaders as they follow Christ.

The old paradigm of leadership is to make people follow. The new paradigm is to make people *want* to follow. Leaders influence—not command. Leadership is all about influence. Leaders who have been influenced by God's Word and God's ways have the ability to influence others to follow. For too long, church leaders have ruled their congregations instead of leading them; or we have told them truth and then made it optional to follow or not follow—as long as they keep attending.

As a result, people aren't convinced to fully and completely obey and follow God's Word. They are consumers. They have an all-you-can-eat buffet philosophy: "I'll take a little of this and a little of that, but none of that please!" In many churches people have no expectation of following their leaders. Their only expectation when it comes to their faith is to consume.

In today's culture, people give up their faith when it fails to bring them greater material prosperity. We need leaders who are willing to give up their prosperity for the sake of their faith; which will, in turn, influence their followers to do the same. I believe that God wants to prosper us for the benefit of His Kingdom which we are part of. However, much of today's consumer-driven faith messages teach that prosperity's purpose is to enrich us personally.

While visiting in Nigeria, an apostolic minister, David Odeyepo, said something that really spoke to me. He said, "Prosperity was not given by God for the purpose of enrichment, but as an entrustment." The prosperity message, without effective modeling and discipleship, leads believers to think that their personal success is a greater priority than the success of God's Kingdom.

DEVELOP AND MULTIPLY

Leading ability is more important than speaking ability (feeding people). We have to do more than just make people feel full—we must also make them followers. I don't mean by force or by rule but by sheer influence. Ministry fruitfulness is determined more by your leadership ability than by your speaking (from the pulpit) ability. God simply will not give you more people than you can lead. Leadership is the key to greater harvest in your ministry or business. For many of us in the Church, we think that the key to great success and harvest is being a great speaker. But some of the most successful pastors and leaders of ministry are not the best speakers. And some of the greatest speakers I know have small or plateaued church membership. Although they continue to perfect their speaking ability, their churches are hindered from growing because leadership issues cost them good people.

For example: I was contracted by a well-known motivational business organization to sell my sermons. They reproduced my sermons onto tapes and I received about 35 cents per tape. They sold my sermons to their Christian leaders, and over the last several years, I've received about $30,000 for my speaking ability. Although I received compensation for my *speaking* ability, they made about ten times more (approximately $300,000) with their *leadership* ability—and they didn't preach one sermon! They built a leader-driven business by marketing training and motivational resources to leaders.

I believe pastors need to work more on their leadership and people skills. That's what I do. I help pastors develop the leader within and in turn develop their followers. That's the apostolic ministry—a ministry of leadership development and multiplication.

LEADING FOLLOWERS

Jesus said His sheep hear His voice and follow (see John 10:27). His sheep don't just feed—they also follow. The head or leader of every church and ministry needs to ask: "How well am I leading?" Are your leaders buying into where you're going? Have you persuaded your sheep or constituency to follow Christ through you? I believe there is a leadership drought in the American Church, but we think, "Man, we sure can preach!" Even though we're ruling and feeding, the sheep are not following or leading.

Pastor, leader, are you being led? Are you *going* anywhere—moving forward? It starts with you. The good news: if you don't have a clue about leadership, you can learn. Learning starts with recognizing the need for leadership and making it your number one priority. We must make following Jesus Christ and leading others to follow Him our first priority. We must embark on a "growth in Christ" journey as did the first twelve leaders. Leadership is about how others are affected when we follow God. When we're truly led, others will follow our following.

Why did the Twelve follow Jesus? Why did they leave their jobs and families to follow Him? Maybe it was because He was the only one *going* anywhere. Others were making noise but they weren't taking people anywhere. I think we're right back at the place where the "religious people" were when Jesus Christ walked the earth. There are too many rules and not enough freedom to become what God destined for us. People are fed up with religion that doesn't transform them. They're stuck in their sin and have lost hope that things will ever get better.

The following questions are meant to stir your thinking about how your life is *going*. Are things getting better for you? Have you got the victory? Are you influenced that God's way is the best way? Have you bought into the truth? Is there passion in your leadership? Are you compelled and compelling to others? Are the leaders in your church working as a team? Do you pray daily? Do you read your Bible? Do you love your mate? Are you free from addictions? Do those in bondage see you splashing around in the river of freedom? Tell me preacher, leader, and Christian do you have the goods? Or have you given up the dream of a victorious fulfilling life in Christ?

We need to go back to the basics in the practice of our faith.

Coaching Followers

I'm very fortunate to live in New England where great basketball, football, and baseball teams are made. This particular season brought new challenges because some star players had moved on. Although the coach exhorted the players who had been champions the previous year and worked steadily with the new players, they lost game after game. Finally, the coach came into practice one day with a basketball and said deliberately, "This—is a basketball."

Church, we need to get back to the very basics of our faith. Are the church leaders leading in the practice of prayer, obedience, humility, fidelity, and leadership?

The greatest need of the hour is the need to lead—not with pretty leadership slogans, sermons, and seminars. Your message is your following. Are you doing what you're preaching? Are others following? Are you leading the way to and through transformation? Change is a process that must take place from the pulpit to the pew.

I think the American Church has turned leadership into an academic subject rather than a lifestyle. There is a mind-set in the political arena especially, that believes leadership is a role people fill in their job, from 9 to 5—but it is different and separate from how politicians live their lives. We've been told by leaders at the highest level "as long as I get the job done, character and morality is a personal issue."

The Pharisees are in control again! They arrogantly communicate that religion is what they should *do*, not who they *are*. Many politicians vote and govern separately from their morality and character. The finger that directs them to self-government and moral self-control is the same finger that pulls the trigger of governmental action or inaction. It's the same finger that pulls the trigger that directs all of their actions both personally and politically. I long for the day when our government leaders will lead us to follow their lives, not just their perceived actions. People recognize insincerity and immoral behavior and will not buy into it—unfortunately, though, they learn to tolerate it and become desensitized to the point of not caring.

In the church setting, others will "buy in" when you as leader are "sold out." Don't try to get others to buy into your message or lifestyle if you don't. It might surprise you to learn that most people in the congregation don't follow the pastor. Most of the congregation will follow the leaders who follow the pastor. Therefore, if your leaders are not following you, the rest of the congregation won't follow you either. If you aren't influencing your leadership, they aren't influencing your congregation. For the most part, the way the congregation lives their lives is the result of church leadership influence or lack of influence.

BASICALLY

We need so desperately to get back to Jesus and the Twelve. He took the time to get His leaders on board. The Twelve were the ones who all others would eventually follow. Because He took the time to lead them, the Twelve followed Him to the end—and in the end others follow the Twelve to Him.

Jesus Christ wasn't an educator. He was a journey taker—the Good Shepherd. Shepherds aren't educators, they're journey takers. Shepherds know that sheep can't stay in the same place and feed. They have to journey on because food is found along the journey.

In Genesis we read how Abraham, Isaac, and Jacob journey to spiritual transformation. We, too, have to take our leaders on a spiritual journey. We must move away from the feed-only (educate) paradigm and become part of the journey to spiritual maturity. Basically, the apostle takes the pastor on a journey. In turn, the pastor takes the church leaders or staff on a journey, who in turn take their leaders along until the entire congregation is following and buying in.

The journey is a process not just a destination. We must develop a process of spiritual maturity that retools and utterly transforms reeds to rocks. The people don't follow the pastor. Most congregants don't see themselves becoming a pastor. In their minds, pastors pray, study, and involve themselves in ministry and do good things because they are paid to do that. Pastors have a conflict of interest. Pastors are good because they are paid to be good. Some think that when the pastor calls to check on them after being absent from services that he's "just doing his job."

But when a leader in the church calls, some think, "Man, that was nice of him to check on me. He's not paid to do that." Pastors are paid to be good but leaders are good for nothing! People in the congregation see an incentive on the pastor's part for their compliance. Many also fear their leader's exploitation. With team-up leadership, more people are involved and there is greater buy in.

But first of all we need to have pastors and leaders who are worthy of a following. Are you living right, pastor? Are your leaders living right? Are they following you? Do they have the vision of the house? Do they have the same core values? Have you taken the time to convince them of your worthy lifestyle, values, cause, and journey?

Jesus Christ took the time to get His leaders on board. They left all to follow Him. They picked up their crosses. When He prayed, they said, "Teach us to pray." He gave and they gave. He gave them an example that He expected them to follow. Do you *expect* your leaders to follow? Is it OK if they don't?

Recognizing the strengths and weaknesses of your leadership team will help you develop it into one that will be a model for the entire congregation. Also, recognizing that you are a spiritual sojourner is a vital part of retooling a top-down leader to a team model. Staff and leadership meetings become more developmental rather than task-focused. The emphasis is on leadership instead of workmanship. Pastors, we need to take the time to define ourselves, decide where we are going, and determine the best way to get the people to want to follow us.

It has been the practice in our ministry to dedicate certain monthly staff meetings for management, and the other meetings focus on growing up the senior leaders so they can develop growth in the leaders they lead, and so on. Building leaders assures a solid team.

ENDNOTES

1. Barnes, Rebecca, and Lindy Lowry. "Special Report: The American Church in Crisis." Outreach May/June 2006. Retrieved 27 February 2007. <http://www.christianitytoday.com/outreach/articles/americanchurchcrisis.html>.

2. http://www.barna.org/FlexPage.aspx?Page=Barna Update&BarnaUpdateID=170.

3. George Barna, "Morality Continues to Decay," *Barna Research Press Release online*, press release, 3 November 2003. Retreived 27 Feb 2007. < http://www.barna.org/FlexPage. aspx? Page=BarnaUpdate&BarnaUpdateID=152>.

CHAPTER 3

Your Team—The Key to Moving Forward

Developing an effective team is crucial when retooling the church. A well-defined team-up leadership model holds team members accountable and provides an environment in which they feel comfortable learning, leaning, and living. Team leadership cannot be vague or ambiguous.

First, the team must recognize and realize the need for working and relating as a team. I realized this need to function as a team when I saw the same problems reoccur. I use this analogy to describe the situation: There is a shepherd (a pastor) wandering around in the desert leading his camels (our problems, inherent weaknesses) through the wilderness. Eventually the shepherd gets to know all the camels and can name each one of them. But the shepherd never delivers the camels (overcomes the weaknesses) because he accepts the wilderness journey as the normal course of desert events. After awhile, not only has the shepherd named the camels but he has named all the offspring as well! When I began naming the grandchildren, I finally realized something needed to change.

Some problems repeated cyclically. One was "staff infections." Someone on the staff had either character or performance issues that negatively impacted or had an unfruitful effect on the ministry. As the top-down leader, it was my responsibility to do most of the correction involving staff ministers. The cycle went like this: When I corrected staff and leaders, it appeared to others that I was unable to get along with some people. I was guilty by association, and correction by unintended design became personal.

Another aspect that made the situation even more distressing was the fact that other leaders on my staff had more in common with the person being disciplined or corrected. Consequently, alliances would be formed that defeated the action meant to solve the problem. Many of the staff had previous negative life and ministry experiences with top-down leaders. Some had been injured by a father, boss, or pastor and could relate more to the one being corrected than to the one doing the correcting. As a result, they pulled back and left the conflict between the "corrected one" and me. This made the correction more personal, lessening the chance of it being received, making it more difficult if not impossible to be accepted. Most people today have experienced top-down leader injuries that can produce an "us against the pastor" situation.

SUBMISSION AND DOMINATION

Most of us learned to be entrepreneurial leaders. Our leadership model was much like a "business starter" leadership model—the boss tells the employee what to do, how to do it, when to do it, and where to do it. So, we pastors tell the church leaders that we're sent by God, so they need to follow, serve, and submit to us. Pastors represent God, not themselves. We think, "I'm the sent one. I have the vision. I see the problems and I have the solutions. I'll take your advice to solve my problems."

This model actually works well for start-up businesses or churches—it works well in its season. Because all of the pressure is at the top, all goes well as long as the leader is well. But when the leader stops, the ministry stops. If the leader is off, the ministry is off.

I'm not saying that there is no need to teach the Church about spiritual authority. We need to teach people to submit to authority because it benefits them to do so. However, we can unknowingly avoid our responsibility of learning to be more skilled and influential leaders if we're not careful. We focus on making people submit, rather than learning to lead them to follow.

In my case, I thought people were obligated to submit and follow me. After all, "I'm their pastor." For years, it never dawned on me that I was inadvertently relinquishing my responsibility to improve my leadership skills by thinking I didn't have to lead them. I believed it was their responsibility to follow me whether they liked it or not. After I taught people about spiritual authority I expected them to follow me—I was entitled to their submission. If they loved God, and unless I was immoral or illegal, they owed it to me to follow and submit. I actually heard it taught that way. I have been confronted many times by well-meaning pastors and church leaders who hold that false belief.

The Bible does not teach a submission that is absent of faith. As a pastor, I ask people to believe in me when I ask them to follow me. They believe that I have heard from God because of the way I live my personal life and the direction I take them as a church.

The Bible does not teach us to not question authority. In fact, we submit to authority better when we question it. We are given the opportunity to not just "give in" but to completely "buy in" to where the authority over us is going. I choose to learn from those in authority: why they do what they do and why they are going where they are going. God doesn't want robots. He wants us to become full-grown sons and daughters.

As a grandfather looking back, I would change one thing about how I raised my Christian children. I would take more

time to influence them to own my Christian values and boundaries instead of taking the short cut of making them give in.
John Maxwell says that the longest distance between two points
is the short cut! Domination is a short cut. We have learned to
take the short cut in ministry leadership. We make people submit instead of taking the time to listen to them and answering
their questions, objections, frustrations, and concerns. We
have mistaken rulership for leadership.

I've learned to welcome challenges to our directives concerning our core values, vision, direction, timing, and over all
ideologies. Listening is my opportunity to decide whether to
change the direction or change the traveling partner. A leader
must take the time to help followers conquer their own inner
conflicts and objections that keep them from following their
leader with their whole heart.

As a leader, I may have spiritual authority but with that
authority I also recognize the weakness of my own humanity.
Others recognize it and are affected by it. Wise leaders
empower their followers to follow them by encouraging them
to vent their objections and then help them overcome those
objections. Only then are leaders able to do the same with
those who follow them.

Leaders who aren't in "spiritual authority" don't view
themselves as having the same advantage as the pastor—to pull
rank and make people submit. Pulling rank can work well for
a godly prophet, dictator or small ministry with a church membership of 300 or less, which is about the size of 80 percent of
churches in the United States. This is not necessarily a bad
model for a godly leader—for the most part it was used to pio-
neer the charismatic movement. It's where most of us are or
were.

There are some exceptions, though. Some very large and
successful ministries have grown to great size and effectiveness

with this top-down leadership model. But after many years, we now see the problems inherent with this model and how they have contributed to where we are in the Church today.

TOP-DOWN LIMITATIONS

Limited buy in. The top-down model of leadership gets a limited "buy in" from the leadership and ultimately from the congregation. Everybody works for the top-lead person—helping the pastor or the top leader do his or her ministry. By the time his leadership influence reaches the pew, there's very little buy in in terms of Christ-likeness, character and morality, core values, involvement, and contribution because people are reduced to consumers who come and are fed (educated) by the "paid professionals." Or as with some ministries, the paid professionals offer their followers a spiritual experience in a kind of "spiritual Disneyland" environment with all the entertainment, lights, and smoke. As consumer-oriented Christians, they are often willing to pay for this experience and/or meal but the average attendee has no long-term intention of following their leader's way or mission in life.

Limited flexibility. The top-down leadership model can cause a leader to seek approval from their followers. This model draws codependents who need someone to tell them what to do. The pastor becomes the caretaker of these needy people who do not intend to change and become disciples, but expect to be fed, entertained, and maintained.

Limited freedom. The top-down leadership model can cause the top-level leader to become isolated, lonely, and tired while keeping the show on the road and handling all the caretaking needs of their constituency. The larger the church grows the more burdensome it becomes. It reminds me of the story of a pastor who was standing on a bridge while his parishioners observed him watching the train go under it. The parishioners asked, "Pastor, we've noticed that are you standing on the bridge watching the train go by. Why?" The pastor said, "I just wanted to see something move that I didn't have to push."

Limited access. The top-down leadership model limits others from learning what their leader thinks and does, as well as how he or she leads. The art of leading is limited to an audience of one. It limits leader reproduction and leaves no successor once the pastor retires or moves on. Dr. Lester Sumerall once told me, "There's no such thing as a success without a successor."

TEAM-UP LEADERSHIP MODEL

In our healthy team model, we:

- Develop everyone on our team to do what we do (execute leadership).
- Live how we live (grow in Christ-likeness).
- See what we see (watch over the flock).
- Recognize what others see (learn from others' perspectives).

The team environment creates an atmosphere and arena where others can inherit and benefit from the team leader's character, experiences, and perspectives. The team leader can then show team members how to do the same with their leaders or followers. Everyone has the opportunity to learn about what it takes to build character and Christ-likeness and how to develop an effective and comprehensive ministry.

The team leader's goal is to reproduce themselves in every person on the team. He or she shares the responsibility and the ownership but doesn't become democratic or consensus-driven. In a church environment, the pastor or ministry leader bears ultimate responsibility to God and has the right to make the final decision regardless of the majority or consensus about the final decision.

The team includes every leader on the team in the process of developing a "vision of the house." Together they determine the values, goals, and purpose of the church house. The entire leadership team buys into the vision of the house and reproduces it among those leaders under them until the goals, core values, vision, purpose and lifestyle is "bought into" from the pulpit. In turn, the vision will permeate through the extending levels of leadership from the pastor or team leader to the pew.

Your leadership team will promote spiritual growth and Christ-likeness throughout the church and create followers who buy into the vision.

Chapter 4

Developing a Reproducible Team-up Model

After recognizing the need to retool your leadership model, you need to develop a top-level team that reproduces leadership in the secondary teams that each member of that top-level team leads.

The following model example is based on my ministry's proven experiences. I share this model with you to encourage and enhance your ministry—ultimately bringing glory and honor to God.

Teams Multiplied

Let's call the top-level team the "First Team." The First Team is comprised of the pastor or executive leader and six members. Each member of this team must lead a ministry in the church such as the music ministry, children/youth ministry, or small groups. The First Team is limited to no more than six ministry leaders under the team leader.

The First Team is the model for all team ministries in the church. As the First Team leader leads (pastor or executive leader), so does the Second Team lead. The pastor leads all teams' ministries in the church through the six leaders. These six leaders in turn develop a team of six leaders who in turn develop six under them.

Why limit the team leader to six leaders on every team? We've found that more than six leaders dilute the team's impact because it doesn't give the team leader enough time and influence with each individual leader. Each leader also needs to spend quality time with the team peers.

The influence of the average pastor over the congregation is very small. Our model encourages a deeper penetration of influence and buy in with everyone on the team. We want the entire First (or top-level) Team on board—then we work at multiplying their teams and influence until their teams are also on board. We continue to reproduce teams down-line until we reach and influence every committed person in the pews.

The team leader includes the team in ministry decision making but bears the ultimate responsibility for final decisions. In our model, we do not make people responsible and then not empower them to make decisions.

INPUT AND OUTPUT

The pastor or executive leader engages every team member on the First Team in ideological interaction (and possibly conflict) while discussing the options, decisions, and actions being considered by the ministry. The team leader collects all input from the team members and develops the options. The team leader makes the final decision only after the dialogue among the team has been exhausted. (Another reason for limiting the team to six people is to minimize dialogue time. The more people on the team the longer it takes to make progress.) The best decisions are made after considering all the options put forth by the team.

As a top-down leader, I was taught that the pastor brought the problem and the solution to the staff meeting. It was his job to explain the problem and everyone else's job to say, "Yep, that's the problem." Then the pastor instructed the staff about their part in carrying out the solution. Each staff person would say, "Yep, that's what I need to do." Since 85 percent of problem *resolution* is determined by problem *definition*, we need to be certain of the problem. Many times in the past we perceived problems that didn't actually exist. I'm sorry to say that we often fixed the wrong problems!

When we were functioning top-down, ministry decisions were limited to the visibility of the person at the top. As that top person, I did everyone's thinking for them. They did what they were told, until I told them otherwise. For instance, if I saw or thought something could be improved, they assumed I would tell them—they had no authority or initiative to offer suggestions, advice, or use their talents or gifts. Although they helped me with my ministry, for the most part, I alone carried the total responsibility for creativity, innovation, and improvement of every ministry area in the entire church.

Because they "worked for me," I wasn't helping them to develop their ministry. The top-down design or structure of my leadership reduced or completely eliminated ownership and buy in from my staff and the leaders who worked with them. Ultimately, this resulted in a loss of buy in at the pew. The staff ministers were doing what they were paid to do. Their incentive or buy in to follow my leadership was financial. And if they did not follow my leadership, they could be fired. In this set up, how could they influence others to follow them or buy into their leadership decisions, ideologies, character, and lifestyle? We can't pay everyone in the church. And we certainly can't fire everyone, although I've seen some churches fire every dissenter.

When functioning in the team model, it becomes the team leader's job to help each team member develop his or her own ministry. In turn, each team member helps to develop the ministries of the leaders under them. Teams multiply down until the lay leaders, who were once the general populace of the church, become team members. The advantage of the team-up model: influence is carried from the pulpit to the pew.

Team members buy in with their participation of opinion and contribution. Buy in means to have a say in the decision making—not that we do just what one individual suggests. After the team leader makes a decision, team members are expected to support the decision as their own even if they don't agree with the final decision(s). In team meetings, every team member's communication and contribution is respected and does not result in a loss of personal significance or in a judgment against them.

Accountability is also different when it comes to the team member. Team accountability is both vertical and horizontal. Each team member is accountable to the team leader as a direct report. However, every member is also accountable to each other for their lifestyle, character, and ministry performance. In addition, they must know each member's contribution to the team and understand its affect on the team. Teamwork is emphasized as opposed to working exclusively for the team leader. Team members are still accountable to the team leader, but we all work together to ensure team success.

On our ministry team, we understand that it takes teamwork to win a Sunday visiting family to Christ and ultimately have that family become part of our congregation. If that family finds a good parking space and is greeted in the parking lot and again upon entering the building, that's good. If a happy-faced volunteer shows them to the nursery and their older children to the children's ministry, that's great. If the ushers help Mom and Dad find an ideal seat near the front but not to close to where we're really cooking, that's also great. If the music is awesome and the worship lifts them into the heavenly of heavenlies, they may begin to consider making the church their home. If the pastor preaches a very prophetic "now" Word of the Lord that confirms the dinner conversation they had the night before, they become convinced. The couple is all set to make us their home. Excitedly the couple goes to the nursery to pick up junior only to find a large knot on their son's forehead. The nursery attendants make apologies, but Mom and Dad aren't coming back! It takes teamwork to minister effectively to people—souls are in the balance.

TEAM DYNAMICS

We lost valuable church families because our ministry failed to help one family with their struggling teenager who had been hanging around with the wrong crowd. This family brought him to the youth service several times but we weren't very friendly to him. At that time, the youth ministry was very unorganized and helter smelters. What happened? The family left our church to look for a better youth ministry. It affected all of us. Mom had played the piano in the music ministry and she quit. Dad no longer served as the head usher. Our kids in the children's ministry missed their children. They wanted to leave and be with their friends in their new church. When one team member fails to do his or her job or responsibility, we all fail! And since a failure affects us all, we all have the responsibility to help each other improve and the right to hold one another accountable for dropping the ball.

In a team environment, *conflicts or performance issues* are dealt with as a team with team awareness and possible team involvement. If it affects the team then the team must be included.

Those who are responsible (for good or bad) share responsibility—not just the pastor. When a failure occurs, that team member or staff minister lets down not only the pastor but also the entire team. And when the team confronts a staff member about performance improvements, it is now a team issue—not a "personal" problem between the pastor and a staff member.

I am not proposing that we become democratic or consensus-driven in our team leading process. The team leader or pastor does not lead by consensus. All team members understand that the one who bears ultimate responsibility to God has the right to make the final decision regardless of the consensus about the final decision. However, such decisions come only after the team members have shared their heart and mind.

There are advantages to *team accountability*. Conflicts and performance issues no longer become personal between the pastor and individual leaders. Also, the pastor or executive leader doesn't appear as dictatorial. The action taken was for the betterment of the team and by the team.

Leaders respond better to peer-to-peer correction than to top-down correction. A corrected leader can't hide under the cover of the pastor's confidential silence while venting his or her side of the story to other leaders. In a top-down structure, unfortunately, one staff leader with a "staff infection" can shut a church down. If the Lord is with you, the setback may only be for several years.

Team correction reduces politics. Corrected leaders who need to defend themselves vent around the team table instead of one-on-one. Any continued defense attempted by the corrected leader away from the team table is viewed as damage against the team—not just the pastor. Team members unite to support the team along with the pastor. So go the leaders—so go the church or ministry.

After instituting team-up leadership, we have had no major setbacks from "staff infections." Correction administered as a team benefits the church and reduces the loss of valuable leaders. At one time, we villainized those I had misled. Now we keep correction out of the personal zone and make it a win-win situation.

What happens when the team doesn't agree with the team leader's decision? I'm not talking about an immoral, unbiblical, or illegal decision. I'm talking about decisions that fall within the vision, core values, and mission of the team (church or ministry). After they have fully voiced their disagreement, it remains the team leader's right and responsibility to make the final decision.

Why do members of the First Team support the pastor or executive leader's right to make the final decision? Because it guarantees their right to make the final decision among the leaders who serve on the Second Team. The Second Team leader or staff minister leads the team in the same way he or she is led by the pastor or executive leader. The model is followed throughout the levels of leadership. The First Team is led by the pastor and his staff or top-level leadership. Each staff member or top-level leader also leads a team of up to six members who in turn also lead a team or ministry. The goal is to develop our leaders and help them reproduce the next generation of leaders.

ALL FOR ONE AND ONE FOR ALL

Second Team members are in submission and service to the First Team. Each team member, like the Knights of the Round Table, offers his or her sword (services, resources, and labor) to serve the First Team first. As a member of the First Team, I lead my Second Team (the secondary ministry team) to serve the First Team. In other words, I don't go to the First Team as a democratic representative of my ministry or the Second Team; and I don't subjugate my Second Team to serve my goals and me. Like Knights of the Round Table, I offer all the services of my ministry team to serve the pastor and his number one team. It's all for one and one for all.

Our future depends on the healthy function of our team. Teams need a model that will bring accountability to how others are led. Models are reproducible only when they are defined.

The typical church focuses on work, events, and maintenance. We don't often recognize the loss of productivity that results from team dysfunction and disunity. We lead and work with a one-on-one mentality instead of leading and working as a team. The Red Sox team would not play good baseball, nevermind *great* baseball, if the team players played one-on-one only with the coach: only the coach pitches to the catcher, only the coach hits grounders, or only the coach catches for the pitchers. Yet that's exactly how we have traditionally functioned in the Church. For the most part, everyone pitches to and catches from the pastor and has no idea what the other team members do or how their job relates to them.

We have to develop as a team and then take advantage of teamwork. Knowing each other's strengths and weaknesses is essential for every team member. Every team member must know the role of the other members and how they can all work together to reach the goal. We can't just work our teams harder and harder as individual employees of the pastor. We must work at being a team—individuals working as one to accomplish the mission and vision of the overall church or ministry.

As mentioned previously, one disenfranchised or offended staff person (a staff infection) can set church or ministry growth back a year or two. It can cost your church thousands of dollars and untold heartache. To avoid this problem, we have to develop a cohesive and reproducible team. During the process of developing a team-up leadership model, certain aspects will arise that need your attention. Take time to address these issues—take time to listen.

Venting

People need to vent objections. For most churches, there's no vent at the top. There's no place for the people under the pastor to voice their objections and differences of ideology leaving the leaders to vent to their Second Team members. They say things like, "I just can't talk to the pastor," or "I don't think what the pastor suggested will work but no one will listen to me." People lose the buy in of any leader when they have no proper place vent. If you don't have a vent at the top, you'll have a blow out or a nagging leak at the lower levels of leadership and within the congregation.

A leader who has no proper place to vent and have input actually offers his or her leader a "give in" not a "buy in." The leader who has been led to think that they have a buy in moves forward mistaking the "give in" as a "buy in" and then wonders why there is no results. It doesn't take long for leaders to realize that their voice is not being heard or taken seriously. This lack of confidence in your leaders will take a toll, especially when important issues arise that require an all-out commitment. Example: stewardship campaigns. Have you ever tried to raise money for a new facility with those who do not agree it is needed? Have you had leaders who hated the proposed building design? Have you had leaders who thought the building design lacked proper functionality?

People must be given the opportunity to speak their hearts and to hear yours. Many leaders are unable to resolve their objections and discouragement because of their fear of rejection or fear of perceived judgment. Allowing them to vent gives them confidence in the gifts God gave them. Your leaders are full of talents and gifts. If they haven't bought into your leadership or the team, they may share some but not all of their gifts with the church. Sometimes you have to have it all (100 percent buy in from leaders) to win a ministry opportunity.

Monty Roberts, author of *The Man Who Listens to Horses: The Story of a Real-Life Horse Whisperer*, sheds light on the subject of leadership. Roberts talks about the loss of potential that takes place in the traditional methods of breaking a horse. After a lifetime of studying horses, Monty discovered their language and is now able to break and ride any horse within 30 minutes. Amazingly, he never beats, intimidates, or scares the horse. He wins the horse over with a buy in from the horse. He completely defies the tradition of domination to break a horse. As a result, he has trained many world champion racehorses.

According to Roberts, about 30 percent of the horse's potential is lost when the horse is broken using the traditionally accepted, brutal, and dominant methods. Roberts now trains business people and educators about his winsome methods with adults and children.[1] We can't raise champions by using methods that make victims. Our leadership is most affective when we take the time to develop the skills that convince followers to follow us.

Conflicts among team members can drain focus and resources from the team. This occurs when team members fund or support the conflict instead of doing what's needed for the team to move forward. Pastors feel the distance from team members who keep their objections hidden. Good leaders can tell when team members give in and don't buy in. We need the buy in at the top because we can only reproduce what's at the top. If they're sold out at the top, then Second and Third Teams can learn to sell out across the board.

As a pastor, I've experienced top-level leaders who stepped back and distanced themselves from me because of their hidden objections or ideological differences. I have watched other leaders with unanswered objections distance themselves from us because my top-level leaders were unable to give them a convincing response. I've sometimes thought, "If I only had equal time to influence them or to benefit from their influence, perhaps my decision would need to change. If I could only get them on board, what a difference we could make."

A team-up model is like the photocopy master, or original. It never gets better than this. Every team is a functional copy of the original. As teams reproduce, we have copies of the original. If there is no defined and established model, the subsequent teams will become distorted. I tell my leaders on the First Team, "It never gets better than us, but it can get worse." Unless there is complete buy in from the top down, the teams degenerate as they are reproduced.

Each team member must enter into agreement or covenant with their relational commitment and accountability with one another. As the pastor commits his life and his ministry to God the Father, so each of the teams needs to commit the success of their life and ministry to Him, ensuring a vital and healthy church moving forward for His glory on earth as it is in Heaven.

ENDNOTE

Monty Roberts, *The Man Who Listens to Horses: The Story of a Real-Life Horse Whisperer* (New York: Balantine Publishing Group, 1996).

CHAPTER 5

MAKING A TEAM COVENANT

Before I recognized that there was no team effort in my ministry, I led in the traditional top-down leadership style. I had a great relationship with each staff member, spanning over 15 years. They all trusted and responded well to me.

Developing and having the same level of trust and accountability with one another, though, was new territory for them. Their relationships were like ingredients in a pot of stew simmering on the stove with the lid on. I took the lid off and then everyone had to deal with whatever had been simmering between them. Some of them were harboring minor offenses and judgments toward one another. Until I took the lid off, they just avoided each other. As long as they got along with the top-down leader, everything was OK.

One of my longest tenured staff ministers came to me and said, "Pastor Ron, I really trust you because you have always been there for me and you have spoken into my life, but I have problems with some of the other staff members."

I was changing the existing dynamics by asking them to expand the relationship they had with me to include one another. At the time, I had no idea that there was anything less than Christian love and loyalty in the house. I truly thought everyone was equal in each other's eyes, as in mine.

The Lord knows how surprised I was at what was simmering under the lid.

Over the years, offenses had come and gone but were never completely resolved. There were silent treaties among staff members. They had accumulated an extensive inventory of misunderstandings, offenses, fears, and judgments toward one another. For the most part, the issues centered on one particular leader who happened to be a close friend of mine. Some believed that this leader had taken advantage of our friendship, hiding behind it to escape accountability. When pressed by other staff members, this leader insisted that he was only accountable to the pastor (me). He didn't agree with the other staff members' critical assessments and believed I was the only one on the team who truly validated and accepted him. He thought the other team members were simply being judgmental.

After listening to other staff members' version of relational conflicts with this particular leader, I asked if they had approached others to help resolve the long-standing conflicts. They had not. Instead, each had individually confronted the leader, but perceiving rejection he responded either in tears or anger. Over the years none of the conflict had been resolved and remained festering beneath the surface of many team members.

I had been totally out of the loop about this situation until I began implementing the new team-up leadership structure. I told this particular leader that he had one week to contact the other team members and resolve the conflict with them or he would be removed from the staff team. Horror filled the leader's eyes. "I don't think I can do that, Pastor." I told him that wasn't an option. We were moving forward into the team model, and we had to be able to resolve our conflicts and offenses with one another so that the other leaders and members of the church could learn how to resolve their conflicts and offenses. I was determined to model a healthy community to the church body. It took a great deal of courage for this leader to follow through—but he did.

LOVE ONE ANOTHER

I believe that if the top-level leaders can't love and forgive each other, there's no hope for the rest of the Church. It doesn't get any better than us. We set the pace in the First Team. If Christians can't love each other how will we ever learn to love sinners? Leadership is influence more than anything else. We influence others to forgive when we are forgiving. We influence others to be forbearing when we are forbearing. That includes being merciful, kind, long-suffering, loyal, and humble. Team-up leadership is about modeling community and Christ-likeness.

After introducing and explaining the team-up model and providing an opportunity for each of my staff member's input, we all agreed with the direction we would take. We agreed that a written covenant was needed that specified how we would relate to one another. We wanted our expectations with one another to be defined. We amended our covenant several times. We may amend it again as we mature and learn to be better at being a "team." We purposed not to be the lid on the church that would lower everyone's experience of community and team. We challenged each other to stretch to a higher standard. Together we drafted the covenant agreement found at the end of this chapter.

Every team member signed the team covenant agreement, trusting the Lord to help him or her fulfill it to the best of their ability. We agree to admit our vulnerability to human weakness and so we ask each other to make us accountable to this covenant agreement. When we think the covenant has been violated, we confront each other individually in love and humility. If a member violates the covenant and it affects the entire team, the team leader decides if it should be brought before the team.

We have had some intense confrontations between team members. When ignoring the conflict is not an option, the problem is resolved. In most cases, individual team members grew closer to one another after intense exchanges and inter-actions. In a few cases, it was necessary for the entire team to confront team members who refused to resolve their conflicts and honor the covenant. To our disappointment, some chose instead to resign. Others had to be asked to resign. We gradu-ally made a major upgrade in staff and leadership retention when we stayed true to the team covenant and model. It took several years to build a healthy, functional team. As a result, staff infections became a thing of the past.

I want you to know that together as a team we accom-plished what I, as a top-down leader, never could by myself. It always grieved me to lose people I loved. I fought regret that I hadn't learned and adopted a team-up leadership style sooner. Every leader we lost because of unresolved conflict took a per-sonal toll on me. We never lost a leader I didn't love. At times, it took months for me to recover. I questioned myself and second-guessed myself.

After you make the decision to introduce, develop, and implement team-up leadership structure, there will be bumps along the journey. People will resist, make excuses, be fearful, or just simply not want to change "the way things have always been." Left unchecked these attitudes will cause friction and conflict. In the next chapter I discuss the next stage of team-up development.

COVENANT AGREEMENT

As a Team Member, I agree to support the team in the following manner:

- **To faithfully attend team meetings and events.** We are a team when we spend time together. We realize our attendance affects others, not only in team meetings but also at important events and regularly scheduled church services. If I don't participate, it says that I don't care and that my presence doesn't make a difference.

- **To be honest and open about my faults, failures, opinions, and ideologies, and to risk conflict when discussing them.** One of the most difficult things to do as a team member is to talk about our weaknesses, faults, and failures openly. Our natural instincts make us self-protective. Self-preservation is a dominant part of our human make-up and to turn these instincts off is no small accomplishment. But that is exactly what is required to be a member of a healthy team.

- **To support and validate the opinions and ideologies of all team members even when I don't agree with them.** In other words, everyone has a right to his or her own opinion and no one will be persecuted for speaking it. The team is a judge-free environment. Nobody is "stupid" or "dumb" for voicing their ideas.

- **To support all team decisions as if they were my own.** Team members will discuss freely all issues and after a decision is made, each person on the team will support the decision, even if they disagree with the final decision.

- **To maintain the bond of unity and peace with all team members by promptly resolving any conflicts and offenses.** Openness and honesty guarantee offenses, but we commit to resolve them in a timely manner. We agree to speak about other team members only what we would normally say about them when at home, to our mates or close friends.

- **To model the team concepts and principles to others.** We realize that leadership is not just academic. We lead by example. Team members become the team leaders for their down-line teams. We will lead others with the same integrity we are led by. We will not take liberties in leading others with a different leadership model than the house team model.

- **To forgive others and myself if we fail to fulfill this team covenant agreement.** We acknowledge that people are human and make mistakes. We say and do things we shouldn't. The grace of God lifts us above human weakness when we repent and ask for forgiveness. We chose to model gracious forgiveness—never punishment toward one another or ourselves.

- **To promptly return communications and carry out action steps previously agreed upon.** We give other members of our team the privilege of proximity. In other words, we receive and return their calls, e-mails, and messages promptly. We take responsibility to do what we agreed to do, when we agreed to do it, unless we communicate otherwise.

- **To be faithful and current in the giving of tithes and offerings to my local church.** We take responsibility to lead by example in our giving. We chose to be a living example of stewardship and prosperity to those we lead and influence. We believe that God only trusts us with spiritual riches when we have first been faithful with unrighteous mammon.

Signed: _____
    Team Member   Date _____

Signed: _____
    Team Leader   Date _____

CHAPTER 6

CURING COMMUNICABLE TEAM DISEASES

There are a lot of great benefits and advantages that come with team leading. When teams are healthy and functional they reproduce healthy and functional leaders.

However, the opposite is also true. Unhealthy, dysfunctional leaders—like families— reproduce unhealthy, dysfunctional team members. Teams are small communities who are vulnerable to communicable diseases. Of course I'm not referring to physical disease as much as relational dysfunction or weaknesses that can be passed from the team leader to others or from team member to member.

I have seen these diseases spread in my own life with those who I am responsible to lead and serve. Being healthy starts with the team leader first.

ME FIRST

During my spiritual journey, the Lord has brought me face-to-face with each and every fault, failure, and dysfunction I had suffered from along life's way. Now those I lead are able to relate to and even learn and benefit from the mistakes, failures, and dysfunctions I've had to face. With God's help, I have found the cure for many of my own dysfunctions.

Overcoming your insecurities and dysfunctions is simply learning to turn your troubles into triumph. For me, the cure started with a ministry/life crisis. Back in the early 1990s, my identity had become attached to the success that I was experiencing in ministry. The ministry was growing and I was "making all the right moves." I felt great about myself. Everyone in the church and on our pastoral staff looked up to me and spoke highly of me. Perhaps I chose to believe that they were all for me and with me. I needed them to like me and believe in me because I secretly harbored much insecurity.

These insecurities were the result of a poor self-image. I fought a daily battle with a lot of negative feelings toward myself. I would fight back in this inner battle to increase my self-worth through my accomplishments and successes. I measured my success by the approval of those whom I loved and respected such as my wife, staff members, leaders, and the congregation.

I finally made it! I was a success. I based my success on the number of people attending our church, the amount of money we received, and by our great new facility with over 30 people on the payroll. We had just moved into a newly renovated 21,000 square foot leased facility located at a very large intersection. Everyone who lived in the Boston area would eventually pass by and see our highly visible ministry building. Our sanctuary area seated more people than other charismatic churches in the area; and we had one of the fastest growing Christian schools on the North Shore of Boston.

Things were going very well. Our sanctuary was filled every time we had a renowned guest minister. On regular Sundays up to 70 percent of our seating capacity was filled. Our Christian daycare and school enrolled over 200 full-time students.

Unknown to me, this entire situation was about to change very quickly. Staff infections sprung up one after another. Then one day a staff member who I had spent years training in ministry became offended with me and left with about 70 people from our congregation to start their own church down the street. I was totally unaware that anyone was unhappy with my actions or me as the pastor.

Without realizing it, I had become infected with the "please disease." Without realizing it, I was so focused on my success and pleasing myself and others that I didn't realize the foundation beneath me was crumbling. I made decisions based on making others like me—I needed their approval.

Through a series of events, including people leaving our church simply to escape the fuss and avoid infection, the church had quite a setback. I felt betrayed, and it wasn't long before church attendance and income fell to an all-time low. It hit me personally like a ton of bricks. I felt like a failure. It seemed like everything I tried to do in the next several years to regain my "success" failed. I just couldn't move past my own personal loss and failure. Every time finances were tight or a particular worship service attendance was low, I would think, "If only so and so hadn't done this or that, I would probably be twice as far along as I am now!"

I thank God for John Bevere's book *The Bait of Satan*[1] that I read in my search for emotional pain relief. What he wrote brought me great relief only after I faced the depth of betrayal and abandonment pain caused by close friends and parishioners.

The revelation of forgiveness from Bevere's book helped me to forgive in great depth. I thought I was finished with the forgiveness subject not realizing that my greatest offender still remained at large—me. I had really let myself down. In my ministry failure, I victimized myself. I used to feel good about myself until I failed. It was then when I realized that I needed to reevaluate my equation of self-worth.

In reading the book *The Search for Significance*[2] by Robert McGee, I realized my equation for self-worth was off—way off. The realizations I made during reading this book changed my life. It's important that leaders are readers. Some weeks I read three, four, or five books. Personal growth and development must be a priority for every leader because we can learn important lessons from others. God has spoken to me many times through the lives of others whom I have read about. I pray that this book about my spiritual journey and transition into team-up leadership will benefit you and all who read it.

INNER REVELATION AND HEALING

I discovered that my insecurity was caused, for the most part, by my search for significance. I had to find self-worth apart from my performance and apart from the other's opinions of me. The Lord was merciful in not moving me forward in ministry until I was healed of this deep-rooted insecurity and dysfunction. As I look back I understand that if He didn't heal me, others would either catch my disease or be hurt as a result of my own woundedness. Since recovering, I have been able to help many pastors and leaders overcome this disease in their own lives.

Painfully I had to admit that I unconsciously exploited and manipulated others to help me succeed. Success was how I thought I could earn love from God, from myself, and from others. Through a process of inner healing and revelation, I rewrote the equation of my self-worth. Until then, my self-worth was determined by the following faulty equation:

My Performance + Everybody's Opinion of Me = My Self-worth.

Now my self-worth is determined by the performance of another—Jesus Christ. He paid for my sins. He gave me a gift of self-worth that I cannot earn. He made me a new creature. I am who *He* says I am. I can do what *He* says I can do.

Like our children, I love them because they are mine. When we first brought them home from the hospital, they couldn't talk, clean their room, or help around the house. Babies contribute and perform nothing more than being the objects of my affection. God loves me much the same way. There is no condition attached to God's love for me. While we were yet sinners, Christ died for us. I finally realized that I'm not what I *do* as a born-again Christian.

If I was to follow the philosophy of what I do is who I am, then I could squat down and bark and I'd be a dog. But no amount of squatting or barking would make me grow a tail and canine teeth. I am what God made me to be. I can't add to that by my performance. I can't build something else of myself.

I now love the person He's making me to be. He's making and molding me into something that looks like Jesus! I have come to accept my value on God's terms. I'm His kid. There's no greater deception than identity deception. What I believe about myself will ultimately be acted out in my life. As a man thinks in his heart so is he.

As a pastor or as a leader, if you don't settle your personal significance issues, you will be tempted to exploit others because of it. I was angry when the failures of others kept me from the success that I thought I deserved. I had taken everyone hostage on my journey to find significance. I made decisions subconsciously that addressed the need I had to be loved. Failure was devastating for me because it reinforced the fear of my worthlessness. My insecurity couldn't handle failure. I had to deny it. To admit my insecurity caused me to react with self-rejection, self-loathing, and self-punishment. I wrongly believed that people who fail should be punished. When I failed I thought God was punishing me by withholding my success and prosperity.

When your identity and performance are welded together, you lack the ability to learn from your mistakes. In life and ministry our greatest gains come only after learning from our mistakes. John Maxwell calls it "failing forward."[3] Saddleback Church Pastor Rick Warren encourages his staff members to make at least one major mistake a week. The only condition is that they not make the same mistake.[4] Only a secure leader can make that statement.

Now I appreciate the value of learning from my own mistakes instead of being devastated by them. Insecure people attach identity to mistakes and miss the opportunity to learn and benefit from them. They are too busy wasting time punishing themselves and others for their mistakes that they stop moving forward.

The worst part of my self-worth crisis was that I reproduced other exploiters who followed my example. They manipulated me because they knew I needed their approval. In my warped thinking, I judged them as villains never realizing they were a chip off the old block. My codependent nature would have been a life-long character flaw had I not recognized and dealt with it.

I asked God to forgive me for being so selfish. I cared too much about what others thought of me. I discovered that the best cure is for circumstances to play out in such a way that others don't like you—lots of others. My "approval addiction" became quite obvious when people began their exodus and many were criticizing me. I had to admit I was making decisions that I thought would make people like me or look up to me for my success. No matter how I reasoned, I was selfish. It was all about me. I wasn't putting God and others first. I was putting "everybody must like me" first. I've learned since finding healing from the "please disease" life is so much easier when there's only one to please—Jesus Christ.

LEADER-TEAM RELATIONSHIPS

You can't lead a team well when you need their approval too much. You have to be able to give and receive love unconditionally, apart from a team's performance. Each member has to be comfortable about saying what they think and feel without having to worry about how it will make you feel about yourself. Productive discussions need to center on content and the subject at hand instead of how comments will upset the emotional applecart of the leader.

When the matter of your self-worth is settled, you don't waste time and resources trying to establish or improve it. When we already love and validate one another on the team, we can move on to the ministry decisions at hand. We can discuss problems without anyone having to fear being blamed or punished for having them.

I use the example of throwing a rod in an eight-cylinder car engine. The old Ron Satrape would have wanted to know who was to blame. Today, though, when accessing the problem, I don't care who was driving. I don't care how fast they were going. I don't care when the oil was changed last. What I care about is how we are going to fix it. Why waste time on finding fault? Finding fault never fixes anything. We may be responsible for our problems but faultfinding is just punishment.

God doesn't punish us. He corrects us. His correction is for our benefit. Correction is the privilege of son-ship. Correction doesn't damage self-esteem—correction builds it. Punishment is payback. Rick Warren says, "When you blame, you're being lame."[5] Thank God for loving us enough to correct us and heal our insecurities! Team members have to feel safe around their team leader and peers. If they aren't confident, they won't risk revealing themselves especially if they witness others being punished for being open and honest. When members remain silent, there is a wealth of ideas that never surface, talents that aren't shared, and hopes unrealized.

In addition to learning how to forgive people and being healed from the "please disease," there are five important healthy relational functions that need to be a part of every team. Author and business consultant Patrick Lencioni calls them the five dysfunctions of a team. Referring to them on the positive side, I call them the *five healthy functions of a team*. I'm not going to go into detail about each healthy function as much as I'm going to share about how we were able to improve our relational health and function as a team.

Healthy relationship function is an essential part of our team-up leadership model. As a result, we can now work toward and hold each other accountable to model healthy relationships. I recommend all leaders read and take your team through Lencioni's book, *The Five Dysfunctions of a Team*.[6] I led my team and have helped other teams achieve healthy relationship function as a result of the principles in the book. It's important to note that dysfunctions are not just separate stand-alone issues. They are interrelated. In other words, one relational dysfunction often impacts another.

As you develop your team-up leadership model, the following five healthy functions of a team will help you define important aspects of interpersonal relationships.

SYMPTOMS OF RELATIONALLY HEALTHY TEAMS

The five symptoms of relationally healthy teams are: a high level of trust, conflict, commitment, accountability, and attention given to results. These characteristics are explained in more detail.

1. *A High Level of Trust.* Trust is having confidence that team members have good intentions toward each other. With trust there is no reason to be protective or careful in the

group. They have learned to be comfortable being vulnerable with one another, without fearing that vulnerability will be used against them. They can openly talk about each other's faults, weaknesses, and failures.

I have worked with many church executive leadership teams—some in small churches and others in megachurches. In every case when healthy team function was defined and discussed, one or more team members chose to leave. In one small church, the pastor and I discussed measuring the level of trust on his team. He assured me that they had a high level of trust because they were a small church and everyone was close and could speak openly with each other. He assured me that on a scale of 1 to 9, they were at least an 8. I warned the pastor that it wasn't normal for a team of any size church to have a trust level that high, having never even worked specifically on building and increasing their trust. He insisted that they were different.

In my experience, churches transitioning from top-down leadership to team-up leadership do not have higher than a 2 or 3 trust level on a scale of 1 to 9. I met with the pastor and his team and defined trust in context to team leadership. We invited everyone to share where they thought the team was on the trust level scale. As each leader talked about their perceptions of the team, the pastor would "tweak" everyone's comments. With the pastor's permission I interrupted his tweaks, emphasizing that the team members were expressing how they really felt. They agreed and thanked me.

Then I explained that when the team leader "tweaks" what the team members have to say, he is communicating that he has to control or adjust their thoughts and words. This tweaking also conveys that unless the team says things a certain way, he won't receive them or like them. Again the team members all agreed with what I explained.

The pastor very humbly thanked me and said, "This is a real revelation." It's important to note that I had a close relationship with this pastor and he trusted me as his pastor. As we continued on with our discussion it was a real eye opener for him. There were trust issues that a few leaders had with him; and there were a lot of other issues they had with each other. If you want others to speak openly (within respectful boundaries) to you and to each other—be ready to receive it. A negative, defensive, personal reaction from the team leader can shut down helpful and important dialogue.

That day the entire team in that church moved up few notches on the trust level scale, but the pastor was feeling really discouraged. I asked him why he wasn't excited about his team members stepping out and saying how they really felt without the fear of being judged or retaliated against. They had made real progress as a team.

"I really thought we were already there," he said. That pastor, like so many others including me, had made the classic mistake of mistaking a "give in" for a "buy in" from their leaders. It takes a lot of courage for people to say how they really feel about issues and ideologies in decision making. Without training and practice in a safe team-up environment it rarely happens. Or when it does happens the truth spoken isn't spoken in love.

As a father I discovered this fact through one of my melancholy (personality temperament) daughters. When my wife or I would have a disagreement or conflict with her or correct her, she would get frustrated to the point of anger and then react. My wife and I would respond, "you can't talk to me that way" and tell her to be quiet. Then she would be upset for days. One day when she reacted at the climax of a conflict with her mother, I said to my wife, "Let her say what she needs to say however it comes out and after it's out we can talk to her about what she said as one subject and then how she said it would be another issue altogether."

It's better to release an offense—even if disrespectfully—than it is to hold it in and poison the person or relationship. Allowing our daughter to "vent" was a breakthrough in our relationship with her. She could find no resolve when we shut her down, which served only to increase her frustration and anger. After we addressed the first issue, then we were able to help her improve her delivery of respectful communications.

Trust is critical to having the kind of conflict that brings resolve and productiveness to a team. It takes a lot of trust to enter the danger zone of conflict without fearing other team members' judgment, criticism, or punishment.

2. *A High Level of Conflict.* Conflict is when team members do not hesitate to engage in passionate and sometimes emotional debate that might otherwise be interpreted as destructive or critical. All great relationships in life are the result of resolved conflicts. Whether it's marriage, family, friendship, business, or ministry, strong relationships are forged in the fires and passion of conflict.

My wife and I have been married for more than 34 years and have had some major conflicts! It doesn't seem to take much to cause offense when you really care about someone. If you don't care, you're not vulnerable. Vulnerability makes injury normal. We're supposed to get offended and then work it out. For people in love conflict is inevitable.

When I preach a sermon on Sunday and someone says, "That was a great message, Pastor," that's OK and I appreciate their comment. But when my wife says the same thing it means more. Why? Because she knows me and has heard me preach for over a quarter of a century. Her perspective is more valuable because of our relationship. If she says my sermon was deficient in some way, it's not a major offense but it's an offense that needs to be resolved. I care about how she measures and sees me. If a visitor offers a criticism, I simply ask what could have been improved.

The closer you are to someone, the higher the risk of conflict. In the church people say things like, "I can't believe they hurt me like that, I thought they were Christians!" My response: "Why not? Why can't you believe that!?" People who love each other have conflict because what they say matters more to each other. You are supposed to have and resolve conflict so that you can have a higher-level relationship. During conflict I discover what is important to my wife. I find out about her core values, what she loves and hates. I uncover her old injuries and help her find healing. I discover her disappointments and help her find hope again. And she does the same for me. I heard someone define intimacy as "in to me see."

Conflicts are like the windows of our soul that others can look into and get to know us. In order to master conflict you have to do two things.

First, separate what you do from who you are. Then you can talk about what you do and how to improve it apart from the issue of personal acceptance and rejection. When improvement is a personal criticism, it's far too painful to endure. We never really improve because improvement is too painful. However, when it's just about what I do then critique helps me improve what I do. We improve our trade skills when we critique our performance.

Second, master forgiveness. Offended people cannot endure healthy conflict. Offended people want to punish others instead of adding to their value through constructive critique. Forgiveness for the Christian is a command.

People aren't always going to package things to your liking in their communications. Team members will get offended and become offensive and defensive at times—it's human nature. Naive Christians need to wake up and realize that we offend people because we're people. Offense is not the issue. Should we offend people if we're Christians? Should we expect that other Christians not offend us?

According to the words of Jesus Christ, "...*it is impossible but that offenses will come...*" (Luke 17:1). Jesus went on to say that if your brother in the Lord offends you seven times in a day and repents, you should forgive him (see Luke 17:4). So why are we surprised and "can't believe" that other Christians offend us? It's the normal human course of events.

So you've been offended? Did the person apologize? Forgive them! Then go to Lowes or Home Depot, buy some lumber, build a bridge, and get over it. Finally, burn the bridge and move on! One of the most important things a team does is model Christ-like character.

In my opinion, the root of all offense is self-offense. The problem isn't about how I treat others; my real problem is how I treat myself. Unforgiveness has its roots in self-offense. Self-punishers punish themselves for their failures and then do the same to others. Forgive yourself. Let Jesus Christ pay for your sins and failures. If I can pay for my sins, then Christ died in vain.

You can't enter into conflict with others when you have unresolved conflict with yourself. When you can't be open and honest with yourself you can't be that way with others. Team members have to be free themselves in order to enter the fray of healthy conflict. We have to be able to forgive quickly, and not hold grudges against others and ourselves. Conflict is a positive thing when ideologies collide and merge into new team decisions. Conflict allows team members to resolve any fears they may have by putting them on the table for discussion before decisions are made. There's nothing more agonizing than being told to do something that conflicts with your heart or convictions, and then not being able to talk about and resolve it or agree to disagree.

With healthy conflict we avoid personality-focused, mean-spirited attacks. With healthy ideological conflict we're able to vent our frustrations or differences of opinion at the top so we don't end up with a blow out at the bottom. Team members must come to the place where they discuss with each other what they used to talk about with their spouses or close friends. Team members should be encouraged to have their say around the team table and not vent it elsewhere in the church and create division or strife.

In the team-up leadership structure, to vent elsewhere is a violation of the team covenant, as you may recall reading the previous chapter. We hold each other accountable not to continue in unhealthy out-of-covenant conflict. If team members are unwilling to abide by the covenant then they are not qualified to lead by example and should step down from their role as a team member. If they are willing but need to learn how, then we take the time to help them assimilate it. We have had new team members added to the team that have mistaken our conflict as strife.

One new team member actually got offended for my wife as I led the team in discussing some issues and decisions. We got somewhat passionate and heated in our exchange, and people interrupted each other (normal, healthy debate for our team). The new team member misunderstood our exchanges and when asked about her first impression around the team table she responded in an offended manner and became offensive toward me, the team leader.

Those who knew the "discussion routine" were surprised at her reaction. They were happy I was there for the team meeting because I travel so much conducting team training and consulting and hadn't been there for some time. I asked if anyone had briefed the new staff member about the team-up model and no one had. No wonder she didn't understand what was going on.

She perceived me as a rude troublemaker. She had no idea that I was trying to "mine out" all the conflict I could in order to get everyone to contribute their more controversial ideas. I was mining for the gold hidden in the hearts of the leaders. I knew some of them weren't on board with the direction we were talking about going, and I was inviting them to admit it and tell us why. You have to make it safe for people to disagree with you and then sometimes you have to go one step farther out of your way to draw it out of them.

People are not naturally comfortable with the risk of conflict. Most are content to quietly pull back and avoid any kind of disagreement that could hurt someone's feelings. The end result is that they can't commit to decisions when they haven't been able to voice their objections. The buy in is not that we do what they say; the buy in for team members is that they had their say—and the team listened. They were a part of the decision-making process. They had their opportunity to inform and influence the decision that was made. After dialogue was completed and the team leader made the final decision, each team member agrees to support the decision as if it were his or her own.

As a pastor with a top-down background I was taught that it was insubordinate for people to disagree with—nevermind debate—the pastor's ideas or decisions under consideration. I was also used to tabling items that created conflict in staff or leadership meetings. I had no idea that in so doing I was avoiding progress and accumulating unresolved conflicts.

3. *A High Level of Commitment.* Commitment is making clear and timely decisions and moving forward with complete buy in from every member of the team, even those who voted

against the decision. Team members leave meetings confident that no one on the team is quietly harboring doubts about whether to support the actions agreed on.

According to Patrick Lencioni, commitment is the function of two things: clarity and buy in.[7] The two greatest causes of the lack of commitment are the desire for consensus and the need for certainty.

When a top-down organization transitions to a team-up leadership structure there is less concern about consensus being an issue. After all, we are used to not voting or having everyone agree before committing to action. However, when a team environment is introduced and people have their say in decision making, we have had to remind people that we're not saying that everyone has to agree with the final decision that is made by the team leader.

The weakness of transitioning to team-up leadership, especially for charismatic folks, is that we tend to go from one extreme to another. We had to make an adjustment with our leaders who wanted to vote on *everything* after they realized that they had a say. Talk about progress slowing to a snail's pace!

As my Baptist father would say, "God sent not a committee because nothing would have gotten done." He said that whenever he didn't agree with a particular decision on the table, he would suggest it be sent to committee. Sending it to committee almost guaranteed its death. Dad said, "They would study that thing and argue over it until Jesus came back!" To eliminate slowing progress trying to have consensus in our decisions, the team leader must make the final decision once everyone has had his or her say.

The next challenge we faced was the need for certainty. Most of us fear failure until we learn to benefit from it. This fear of certainty causes analysis paralysis and can produce a lack of confidence within the team. For the "ready, fire, aim" people, this is not a problem. But when the melancholy detailed and deep thinkers get involved, it's a different story.

I've worked with many frustrated pastors who have team members trapped because they fear certainty. "It seems like it takes an act of Congress to get anything done around here," they tell me. Bureaucracy is the unintended result of the need to be "over certain" before decisions are made. Talk about a progress stopper! This is the kind of thing that burdensome maintenance mechanisms are made of. Whether it's voting or planning, either one can keep a team and an entire church from making decision-making progress. After decisions are made, clarified, and defined, the team can hold each other accountable to execute those decisions.

4. *A High Level of Accountability.* Accountability is the willingness of team members to call their peers on performance or behaviors that might hurt the team. This is perhaps one of the most difficult things for leaders to handle. When we started working on this aspect of retooling with our team, they were really challenged. They were accustomed to me confronting staff members about performance or behavioral issues. It's a real turning point for a team member when they muster the courage to confront another team member—especially if it's a team member with a strong personality.

I've noticed that there are two types of leaders when it comes to confrontation. Leaders who don't like to confront at all and leaders who confront too much. Each type has to make some adjustments. One leader has to learn how to pull the trigger and just do it. The other one has to learn not to pull the trigger too much or too often. In the book, *One-minute Manager*, the author says that leaders need to correct others in a way that after being corrected, they think about their own behavior instead of the one who corrected them.[8] In other words, they don't hide their inappropriate behavior behind our corrective-measures behavior.

This pastor-only discipline style was the cause of major dysfunction for our ministry. In the top-down leadership model it was my responsibility to correct problems concerning the church leaders and staff. When one leader shoulders an unfair burden of the correction that person becomes the "common enemy." Eventually, most, if not all, of the leaders and staff members will have had some major confrontation or minor correction by the "disciplinarian" and it becomes personal.

In the team-up leadership model, team members hold each other accountable for their performance and behaviors. People receive peer correction better because it isn't seen as a personal attack. During the time we were implementing this new discipline strategy, there were a few rough situations. If a staff person balked at the correction by the team and got upset and quit, it wasn't just "another person who couldn't get along with the pastor" and had to be fired, it was the result of that person not receiving the correction of the team.

If the disenfranchised staff member left the meeting and tried to negatively influence others, the other team members communicated the truth of the situation with those in their circle of influence. I wasn't alone defending myself to others who felt sympathy for the "wounded leader." In fact, because of this new dynamic, I am now in a position to talk to those involved and ask them to forgive each other, if that is what the situation warrants. After curing this staff infection, our ministry moved up to a new level of relational healthiness.

I've noticed that leaders with the greatest potential are sometimes our greatest challenges.

Most great leaders come in raw form. In a team environment they can mature and fulfill their destiny in Christ. If leaders don't accept discipline they will eventually become immune to it.

For example, I had been helping a pastor out west transition his top-down led megachurch to a team leadership model. He called me one day very excited.

"Pastor Ron, this team thing is really working. One of my First Team members had some performance issues and the other team members confronted him to see if they could help him improve. He got angry and said that he didn't have to answer to them. They told him that he does now because they were a team. They were humble but firm and loving. He got so upset with the team that he cursed and quit right on the spot."

The pastor and team leader tried to reconcile the leader to no avail. What the pastor was excited about was the fact that there was no negative fallout in the church toward him or his wife. The team handled the correction and for the first time the anointing was protected and correction became a team responsibility. Before retooling their leadership structure, the pastor and his wife would have to go into seclusion to figure out how to best handle this type of staff departure situation. Not this time. This time, the *team* came up with a proposed plan. One of the team members assumed that area of relinquished responsibility and actually did a better job.

Other team members have since come and gone at that church but the team only gets stronger.

Staff changes have a tendency to weaken people's confidence in a top-down organization. I have been heartbroken many times when we've lost really good people because we lacked the leadership mechanisms or model to lead them. I could never return to top-down leadership after seeing the benefit it brings to everyone. In the kingdom of God people are not expendable; they are precious and important to God and to me. I would like to rewind the tape of life and redo some of what we did wrong. I hope you learn from our mistakes. I know we can't rewind the troubles we had in life; but we can fast forward. In other words, move forward faster by eliminating setbacks and learning from our mistakes.

5. *A High Level of Attention Given to Results.* "Attention given to results" means to focus seriously on achieving specific objectives and producing clearly defined outcomes. Healthy teams make each other accountable for successful results. We must be focused on winning new converts and multiplying disciples, leaders, ministries, and churches. And we must be ruthless about it! We don't have time to dilly dally around with anything short of what God commanded of us. Only when we bear much fruit do we glorify the Father.

I'm amazed at how little results matter in the average American church. In my observation, most churches are stuck in the maintenance mode. Most lack a clearly articulated vision, defined core values, or defined DNA. In fact, many churches seem to play reruns of previous services every Sunday.

Unfortunately, there are a great number of churches that lack an action plan or calendar of events that commits them to carrying out their vision and goals. There are no real leadership processes, systems, and structures in place that moves them forward toward real harvest and progress.

Leaders in the local church must realize that if they have no real defined identity, direction, and structures in place moving them into the future they will stagnate indefinitely. All they have ever been is what they will forever be. This staff infection sometimes stems from the top. I venture to say that a majority of church leaders find fulfillment solely in having a noble call and vocation. They are content where they are.

I have noticed that many in ministry have subjugated the purpose and goals of the church for their own personal goals or to meet their need for significance. They are in ministry to teach or preach or to do their own ministry. But preaching and teaching and being a "man or woman of God of faith and power" is not solely what the Church is about.

Jesus Christ gave specific commands and directives. He didn't make requests. It's the great *commission* (command), not the great *permission*. Have we forgotten that our Jewish Father God is results oriented? He is the husbandman who purges and prunes the vine to increase its fruitfulness. He's the God who sends stewards to hell for burying their talent.

Jesus is the Lord of the Harvest. He's the Shepherd who leaves the 99 sheep to find the one lost. Jesus said, "...*I do always those things that please the Father*" (John 8:29). Jesus also said, "...*for this purpose the Son of God was manifest, to destroy the works of the devil*" (1 John 3:8).

What has happened to the Church and her leaders that we've subjugated heavenly goals and purposes for our own earthly goals and purposes? We want people to look up to us. We want to be important. We want to do our thing, in our way and on our terms. Where's the nobility in those things?

The ultimate team dysfunction is when we don't care whether people make it to Heaven or spend eternity in hell. If I don't have a Holy Spirit-inspired written vision, goals, and action plan for how we're going to reach and make disciples for Christ, it's all about me by default.

God doesn't look the other way when a pastor reaches a plateau in his leadership ability and can't grow a church past 200 members. Pastors are commanded to reach the world—don't be content to stay where you are until Jesus Christ comes back.

CHURCH PLANTING

If you have faith for a 200-member church, then multiply that faith in another location within a 50-mile radius of your home church. There is no need to turn your church over to someone else and start over. Raise up a leader within your team to lead the home church with you, then start another church utilizing all your home church resources.

Make your home church a church-planting church. Make every church you plant a church planting church. Transition your ministry into an apostolic multiplication ministry. I believe God called every pastor to be an apostle. You are an apostle who hasn't grown into the mantle yet. You don't automatically become an apostolic leader just because you planted a church, though. You're still a pastor until you move from *addition* ministry to *multiplication* ministry.

You have the opportunity to transition into the apostolic when the church you currently pastor transitions into a church-planting church. Reproduction and multiplication is one of the defining characteristics of the apostolic. Whether it's what you are teaching or what you are leading, you becoming apostolic when the math in your ministry changes from addition to multiplication.

The Lord spoke to me one day in a quiet time of prayer. He said, "You are not ruthless enough to accomplish my will for your life." I had a hard time with the word *ruthless*. To me it sounded inappropriate—it challenged my theology. God is a loving God. So how could God be a ruthless God? He couldn't ask me to be something more than He could be...could He?

The Lord revealed to me that He was ruthless when it came to fulfilling the will of the Father. Jesus made absolutely no compromises when fulfilling His mission. At that time God was revealing this to me, I was allowing my loyalty to people and my friendships to keep us from doing what God had called and purposed us to do as a church.

One thing I've learned about the nature of God—He's not comfortable or OK with losing. Why are many of us in the

Church so indifferent about winning and losing? If we are going to win the spiritual battle ahead of us and reap a global harvest, then we are going to have to be more ruthless about fulfilling our purpose.

If you don't know how to do that, then pray and get help from those who do. I have helped many teams of pastors and their leaders define themselves and incorporate cutting-edge leadership processes, systems, and structures into their churches. Many teams who have followed through with what we developed have multiplied their teams and leaders in just a year.

Let's cure all the communicable diseases plaguing our churches, leadership teams, and congregations. Let's forsake the lure of ministry "status" and accomplish something that really matters to the glory of God. Let's leave a legacy in the Kingdom of God that continues long after we have gone home to glory.

ENDNOTES

1. John Bevere, *The Bait of Satan* (Lake Mary, FL: Charisma House, 1994).

2. Robert McGee, *The Search for Significance* (Nashville, TN: W Publishing Group, 1998).

3. John C. Maxwell, *Failing Forward: How to Make the Most of Your Mistakes* (Nashville, TN: Thomas Nelson, 2000).

4. Warren, Rick. "How Do You Handle Staff Mistakes?" Rick Warren's MinistryTookBox. 9 May 2001. Retrieved 27 Feb 2007. < http://www.pastors.com/RWMT/?ID=8&artid=286&expand=1>.

5 Warren, Rick. "How Do You Start Over Once You've Failed?" Rick Warren's MinistryToolBox. 13 June 2001.

Retreieved 27 Feb. 2007 < http://www.pastors.com/RWMT/?ID=13&artid=405&expand=1>.

6. Patrick M. Lencioni, *The Five Dysfunctions of a Team: A Leadership Fable* (San Francisco: Jossey-Bass, 2002).

7. Patrick M. Lencioni, *The Five Dysfunctions of a Team: A Leadership Fable* (San Francisco: Jossey-Bass, 2002).

8. Kenneth Blanchard, Ph.D. and Spencer Johnson, M.D., *The One Minute Manager* (New York: William Morrow Company, 1982).

CHAPTER 7

YOUR MINISTRY PATTERN

As team-up leadership models are reproduced they form a pattern in subsequent leadership model production. A defined pattern brings accountability to leadership concerning cohesion and conformity of house vision and core values.

Patterns are important. Everything that's made in a modern society is made according to a reproducible pattern. For example, buildings and clothing all are built or made according to patterns. The charismatic church, on the other hand, goes from week to week without a defined pattern. We think we're being spontaneous or led by the Spirit, when in actuality repeat over and over what we experienced in our past.

One of the major crises that we face in our society is the loss of our God-given societal patterns. The pattern that worked to populate the planet was Adam and Eve, not Adam and Steve. Problems plague us when we think we know better than God how life should be lived—or how worship should be done, or how families and churches should be constructed.

God has a pattern for creating and developing all of creation. He has a pattern or plan for all that He does. When we follow His God-given pattern we get God-given results.

The heavens are built according to a pattern. The tabernacle and all its contents were built according to a pattern. God continues to give us patterns for ministry and business development. Over the years He has led our ministry in pattern development that ultimately made us who we are today as a Christ-like people and ministry.

"*According to all that I shew thee, after **the pattern** of the tabernacle, and **the pattern** of all the instruments thereof, even so shall ye make it*" (Exod. 25:9). A pattern brings accountability when we would like to do our own thing. To me the tabernacle refers to the place of ministry and the instruments refer to the people who are the instruments of His praise.

God cautioned them to follow the pattern He had given to them:

> *And look that thou make them after their pattern, which was shewed thee in the mount* (Exodus 25:40).

> *And this work of the candlestick was of beaten gold, unto the shaft thereof, unto the flowers thereof, was beaten work: according unto the pattern, which the Lord had shewed Moses, so he made the candlestick* (Numbers 8:4).

To not follow the God-given pattern was rebellion:

> *Therefore said we, that it shall be, when they should so say to us or to our generations in time to come, that we may say again, Behold **the pattern** of the altar of the Lord, which our fathers made, not for burn offerings, nor for sacrifices; but it is a witness between us and you. God forbid that we should rebel against the Lord, and turn this day from following the Lord, to build and altar for burnt offerings, for meat offerings, or for sacrifices, beside the altar of the Lord our God that is before his tabernacle* (Joshua 22:28-29).

To not follow or misuse the pattern was considered rebellion. David gave the God-given pattern to Solomon to build God's house. Solomon was accountable to follow the pattern.

*Then David gave to Solomon his son **the pattern** of the porch, and of the houses thereof, and of the treasuries thereof, and of the upper chambers thereof, and of the inner parlours thereof, and of the place of the mercy seat, And the pattern of all that he had by the Spirit, of the courts of the house of the Lord, and of all the chambers round about, of the treasuries of the house of God, and of the treasuries of the dedicated things…And for the altar of incense refined gold by weight; and gold for **the pattern** of the chariot of the cherubims, that spread out their wings, and covered the ark of the covenant of the Lord. All this David said **the Lord made me understand in writing by his hand upon me, even all the works of this pattern*** (1 Chronicles 28:11-12;18-19).

Notice that God's hand directed David in the development of His pattern.

God's hand is again directing apostolic leaders and business people to build the Kingdom for the glory of God. When they restored God's glory to His house, they restored God's pattern according to Ezekiel 43:10: "*Thou son of man, shew the house to the house of Israel , that they may be ashamed of their iniquities: and let them measure* **the pattern**."

PATTERN IMPORTANCE

Some years ago I realized our ministry had no pattern or process for developing disciples or leaders; consequently, people weren't changing or becoming Christ-like. I was ashamed and frustrated because we had no pattern of accountability.

God wants to establish His pattern in us so others will believe. Discipleship is a pattern-making ministry. "*Howbeit for this cause I obtained mercy, that in me first Jesus Christ might shew forth all longsuffering, for a pattern to them which should hereafter believe on him to life everlasting*" (1 Tim. 1:16).

As a believer raised in the word of faith movement, long-suffering didn't fit my theology. Suffering was "of the devil." My pattern was faulty from the start. For years I felt like a failure every time I suffered a loss or felt the delay of God's blessing. I didn't realize that God's agenda was different from mine. He was more concerned with my character development than He was in my apparent "success." I was ready for harvest and prosperity in my current condition. I wanted unsanctified ministry on my terms. Don't get me wrong. I believe God wants us to prosper and succeed. That is why He develops our character and Christ-likeness. It takes a lot of character to endure wealth. Once again, I'm reminded of what a Christ-like apostle from Nigeria said to me, "prosperity is not for enrichment, it's an entrustment."

God also uses patterns to reproduce leadership. "*In all things shewing thyself **a pattern** of good works: in doctrine shewing uncorruptness, gravity, sincerity*" (Titus 2:7).

My pastor, Steve Vickers, says, "Ministry is not a work I do for God, it's a work God does in me. I am the work of God." God does a work in me while I'm serving Him in the ministry. I realize ministry is work but it's not all the work that's going on. God is more importantly working on our character and Christ-likeness. He is establishing a pattern in us from which others can be reproduced. God's covenant is a pattern. The old covenant was a shadow of the new. In the new covenant, Christ is the pattern God uses to build Christians.

> *Who serve unto the example and shadow of heavenly things, as Moses was admonished of God when he was about to make the tabernacle: for, See, saith he, that thou make all things **according to the pattern** shewed to thee on the mount* (Hebrews 8:5).

The Old Testament sacrifices were patterns of the New Testament sacrifice of Jesus Christ. Old Testament animal sacrifices required the use of blood and were a pattern or

shadow of the blood of the Lamb of God in the New
Testament.

> *It was therefore necessary that **the patterns** of things in the
> heavens should be purified with these; but the heavenly things
> themselves with better sacrifices than these. For Christ is not
> entered into the holy places made with hands, which are the
> figures of the true; but into Heaven itself, now to appear in
> the presence of God for us:* (Hebrews 9:23-24).

God also uses covenants or patterns to design creation and
days, and seasons are governed by it.

> *Thus saith the Lord; If ye can break my **covenant** of the day,
> and my **covenant** of the night, and that there should not be
> day and night in their season; Then may also My **covenant**
> be broken with David My servant, that he should not have a
> son to reign upon his throne; and with the Levites the priests,
> my ministers. As the host of Heaven cannot be numbered, nei-
> ther the sand of the sea measured: so will I multiply the seed
> of David my servant, and the Levites that minister to Me*
> (Jeremiah 33:20-22).

God's *pattern causes multiplication* of His chosen seed.
Apostolic ministry is an anointed multiplication ministry. The
majority of the present local church patterns are addition ministries. They add a few people now and then. God's pattern,
though, is multiplication. Why does God use a multiplication
pattern? The world is multiplying; we can't reach them with
addition. God is already committed to multiplication since He
first created Adam and Eve. He is accountable to the pattern
He has already established.

> *Thus saith the Lord; If my **covenant** be not with day and
> night, and if I have not appointed the ordinances of Heaven
> and earth; Then will I cast away the seed of Jacob, and David
> My servant, so that I will not take any of his seed to be rulers,
> over the seed of Abraham, Isaac, and Jacob: for I will cause*

their captivity to return, and have mercy on them (Jeremiah 33:25-26).

It is important to notice that God's design for His family (the Church) is connected to the design of nature itself. The integrity of God's spiritual patterns is just as sure as the sun rising tomorrow or the seasons changing each year.

THE NEED TO DEFINE PATTERN

Every God-called ministry has its own unique pattern design. Unless you start a church or have founded a ministry, most pastors and leaders inherit patterns (good or bad) that have evolved over the years or have been absorbed from the main church or organization. Defining patterns is the first step to correcting or enhancing them for the betterment of the ministry.

I first became aware of our need to develop our own defined ministry pattern after certain problems kept reoccurring. For instance, we had a hard time successfully attracting pastoral staff from outside our group of churches. Like most ministries, we also had more success hiring from within our existing leadership. Before implementing our team-up leadership style, we didn't know how to develop and multiply our own leaders so we would have the future leaders we needed.

A few years ago, two smaller churches in our area merged with one of our churches. Unfortunately, these mergers were not successful long term. As we reflected on it later, we realized that there were more differences than likenesses for those outside of our ministry to accept easily—especially since we had no defined identity for the new members to buy in to. We needed a defined identity so that others (churches and leaders) who were like-minded could assimilate.

Rather than assimilating, several of the merged pastoral staff members actually thought that we should be absorbing and adopting *their* way of doing church. It was not their fault as much as it was our ignorance about the need to define ourselves. After our last failed staff member assimilation, my pastor (who is a member of our board of directors) asked me, "Ron what did you learn when this didn't work out?" I became defensive knowing that this was not our first failed attempt at hiring top-level staff members.

First, I tried to pin the failure on the staff member who wasn't able to get along with others in the church. He had certain problems that weren't noticed initially that resulted in me making a change. I was ready with a "what was wrong with him" list but that didn't answer the question my pastor was asking.

"Ron, I didn't ask what was wrong with the person. I asked what did you learn when you hired him and it didn't work out?" Now I'm starting to feel a little guilty. I failed the church because I hired the wrong person and it caused problems. Pastor Steve picked up on my feelings and said, "Let me make this clear Ron, the Lord led you to hire that person, he didn't work out, and he wasn't supposed to work out so you could learn something. So what did you learn?"

I wasn't ready for that question—it challenged my theology. I thought pastors were supposed to pray and hear from God and do what God led them to do. As long as they heard from God they would always make the right decisions. Whenever wrong decisions were made it was because they missed God. You know what I mean, everything is supposed to be black or white—right? And then there was the timing thing that could mess us up when we got ahead of God.

This situation (failure) taught me that God wants us to do more than just what we're told to do. Doing what we're told to do is a good starting place for the immature; but He wants us to grow up and learn how He thinks and discover the process that He uses to do what He does. You can't learn how to be an architect by just hammering down nails. We have to learn the process behind what God (the spiritual Architect) does—then we can change, reform, or reproduce the pattern as the world and cultures around us expand and change.

Many if not most denominational churches are still doing church like people are living in the days of Christ or in the days of the Protestant Reformation or the Pentecostal or charismatic movements. Our culture and even language have continued to evolve, and we need to retool our churches to reach people today with the Good News. Our message is sacred and we can't change that. But our methods aren't sacred and we must adapt to reach as many people as possible.

Neighborhoods are being transitioned as the economy impacts their cities. Immigration brings another kind of change to cities and towns. God is raising up spiritual architects (apostles) who are willing to learn divinely inspired processes for transforming people, towns and cities, regions, states, and nations.

For me, realizing that other like-minded church leaders had a hard time seeing the purpose and pattern of our church meant that there was a major deficiency and weakness in the way we were functioning as a ministry.

I took Pastor Steve's question back to our staff meeting and asked them what they thought God wanted us to learn from this situation. No answers. I asked for a show of hands how many knew that Pastor So-and-So (who had come on staff about two years earlier) wasn't going to make it with us long term. About a third of them knew he wouldn't make after about six months. Some knew it after three months, and my secretary knew it after about two weeks!

The next big question: "How did you know that he wouldn't make it?" They all had the same answer though worded a bit differently. "He wasn't like us!" "He didn't do things like you did them, Pastor Ron, or like you've taught us." "He doesn't represent the ministry well."

This is when the light went on. Because we did not have a defined ministry identity, "outsiders" were at a disadvantage. If they had a way of knowing who we were to begin with, they may not have come on board in the first place—or they could have had the opportunity to buy in to our core values and successfully transition in with us.

As we talked about it more in our staff meetings we realized how often this problem had occurred over the past several years when it came to lost or dismissed staff and leaders. When we don't define our ministries, others will redefine them for us.

Although there were unwritten core values, patterns, and processes for who we were and how our ministry operated, no one else knew them because they weren't defined or documented. We only knew what they were when people didn't fit in and we blamed them for not getting on board with us.

Undefined core values are also misleading—intentionally or unintentionally. It is tempting to morph into a ministry that caters to what people need at the moment. That way they will join the church, serve in the ministry, and give their money. Some may consider this as "evangelistic," but it is misleading— especially when they haven't been made aware of the ministry's core values. When challenged, they become completely disarmed and their reaction is perceived as non-conforming or even rebellious. In reality it was a set up from the start.

I'm not referring to doctrine—our church has always been very clear about our doctrines. Our culture, core values, and patterns lacked definition. People are often more affected by those issues than they are about doctrines.

DEFINING MINISTRY PATTERN

Defining your ministry pattern begins with a pastor or apostolic leader who, through Holy Spirit revelation and years of ministry experience, helps you identify, define, develop, and implement a proven and successful ministry pattern. Other leaders in his or her house or ministry can then follow that leader and reproduce the house pattern and inherit the same or better ministry results. The apostolic anointing flows through those who follow their apostolic leader.

God blesses those who follow the pattern of their house. Patterns are for the purpose of reproductive inheritance. Without a defined and occasionally redefined pattern, the ministry loses its definition each time its leader dies or the ministry is reproduced through others. Without a defined pattern, if the visionary leader departs, the people may too quickly forget the who, what, why, where, when, and how of their ministry calling.

A written pattern and understanding of its process assures the integrity of the original apostolic DNA. The lifetime of a ministry is longer when future leaders can continue to see and value what the founding leaders saw and valued. They must understand the original ministry pattern process, not just legalistically follow the written pattern of ministry. They must learn to be ministry architects who continue to design the future without alienating or losing the integrity of past ministry design. They can then segue from what was to what is to what is to come. I liken it to Boston's skyline, you find a mixture of architectural design that reveals the city's heritage and historical past that was foundational to its present-day greatness.

We learned how to define our pattern by looking through the rearview mirror of our ministry. Although we hadn't clearly defined ourselves, we raised up leaders who somehow caught it and became fruitful and successful. We realized as we discussed our ministry pattern that those of our leaders who did their own thing or copied someone else failed to be fruitful and resulted in a disconnection from the blessing of God for them. Some leaders had inadvertently sowed a divisive pattern into our ministry that caused confusion and division—as though our body parts belonged to someone else. It was more serious than staff infections; there were abnormal growths like cancer that infected others and in some cases caused the death of ministries.

Apostle Paul was a wise master builder who developed the patterns that others followed and reproduced with fruitful results. We see the patterns in the gifts of the Holy Spirit in First Corinthians chapter 12. We see them in the fruit of the Spirit written about in the Book of Galatians. There are Israeli tribal patterns in the Old Testament and the apostolic pattern of twelve in the New Testament. In the Book of Acts we can see the early Church followed a pattern of growth. Apostolic and prophetic patterns of ministry are returning to the Body of Christ as the Holy Spirit prepares the Church to network for global Kingdom expansion.

I believe the Holy Spirit is breathing on the Church newly revealed apostolic patterns of ministry that will vary in different places but will have the ability to connect and unite the Church globally in the near future. The prophetic ministry will be critical in this development as well. Like the Internet we will all plug in someday and be one great Church in Christ. We'll be able to share all that we have together for the furtherance of the Kingdom of God! Great inheritance will result when the worldwide apostolic networks unite. The variety of these new apostolic patterns will not conflict with each other but will include different kinds of giftings, anointings, and administrations. They won't alienate or illegitimize the historic church but instead include and build upon it.

In my experience, our ministry has been hindered in the past when we brought in leaders in the higher levels who don't learn and follow our house ministry pattern. They ended up confusing and hindering the work of God. Now we take the time and effort to train every pastoral leader in our ministry so they understand and follow these defined patterns:

- Order of Worship Service.
- Small Group Ministry.
- Leadership Development.
- Interchurch Ministry.
- Communication.
- Discipleship.

New members and upcoming leaders are also trained to understand and follow the pattern as they engage in ministry with us. As we grow and leadership advances through the ranks, the pattern normally diminishes somewhat. Vision degenerates and must be refocused to the pattern. Apostle Paul observed their order even in his absence. He obviously had accountability structures in place that maintained pattern integrity.

WHAT WE LOVE AND HATE

In developing our own unique pattern of ministry we realized that two things tell us what's important to us—the things we love and the things we hate. Loves and hates are the trigger points of our core values. "What I love about this church" was a good place for us to start as we began the process of developing our ministry pattern.

If you're starting a new ministry, ask yourself, "What things would make me love a ministry?" What causes passion to ignite when you talk about a ministry that you love? Six other leaders on our executive team and I sat around a table and we all chimed in and talked about what we loved about our ministry. For example: we love charismatic worship, ministry of the Word, Christ-likeness, and affective leadership. We found certain emphases were common among us as we talked about different aspects of the ministry. The ministry's core values had been "unofficially" defined over the years, but now it was important to talk about, identify, define, and agree together what our ministry pattern and core values are.

Then we talked about what we hated to see happen in the ministry. For example, we hated relationships to be impersonal and irrational. We hated to lose good people when it wasn't necessary. Pattern characteristics began to materialize as we searched our hearts for what God had placed there. We were on an exciting journey of discovering who we were, and in doing so we would tap in to our God-given passions and dreams. Who we are was in us, all we needed to do was draw it out. Over the years we had unconsciously been drawn together as we gravitated toward certain core values.

The other leaders weren't just submitting to my leadership; they had something in them that the Holy Spirit had placed in them for such a time as this. We all sensed a definite appointment with destiny, and we were finally coming to it. A particular Scripture seemed to confirm what we all were experiencing: "*A plan in the heart of a man is like deep water, but a man of understanding draws it out*" (Prov. 20:5 NKJV).

We continued talking until we developed a comprehensive and complete ministry pattern that finally defined who we were. Finally we had a pattern that we could present to our existing constituency, future membership and leadership prospects, as well as ministry associations.

We agreed to review the pattern at regular intervals should there be a need to make any changes or improvements that we sensed the Lord was revealing to us. Sometimes vision comes in installments. We wanted to have some fluidity knowing that the Lord could, as He had in the past, lead us to make improvements and changes.

My role now was to act as the team leader and facilitator who would draw out what God placed in us individually as well as collectively. I wasn't the top-down leader telling everyone our vision and core values anymore—I was part of the team-up leadership.

Because all of the other staff members were participants in the discovery process, the vision, core values, and pattern that emerged became our own. God had called us to be together and seeded something in us that needed to be drawn out by the Holy Spirit through apostolic and prophetic leadership.

Now I have the opportunity to lead other pastors and apostolic leaders through the same process with their leaders. I don't go to their ministry to make them like us. I help them to discover who they are. Together we take the journey of discovering and defining their unique identity, DNA, and ministry pattern.

MINING FOR GOLD...OR NICKEL

I believe the Body of Christ is plagued with sameness. I'm tired of the same old "church growth" mechanics that I used to bring home from a conference and try to assemble here in New England. I tried to be someone else only to be frustrated and fruitless. Success in ministry is not a program that can be imported from someone or somewhere else. Success is mining out what God has already placed in you and cultivating it.

I tried unsuccessfully for years to build a megachurch in New England. I was distracted, though, by the success of other ministries in Alabama, Oklahoma, Florida, and Phoenix and was enticed by their vision and harvest. I was willing to try just about anything to get similar results. As a result, I ignored my own ministry identity in trying to be like them. I looked everywhere for the answer to how to build a megachurch—except in my heart and the hearts of those who God placed around me. The answer was with me all the time.

This revelation reminded me of a story I heard about a family in Massachusetts who lived on a farm during the days of the gold rush in California. The farmer had toiled many years on the farm to make only a meager living. He had a typical old New England farmhouse with a white picked fence around the front yard. The fence gate, like the rest of the house, was in need of repair because it dragged on the ground when it was opened or closed. Well, at the insistence of the farmer, the family packed up, sold the farm, and moved to California to mine for gold. They never did strike it rich but the person who bought their farm was a mineralogist who, upon fixing the fence gate, noticed that the ground where the gate scraped had become shiny from the wear. The new owner had the substance analyzed and it was found to be nickel! As a matter of fact it was one of the largest nickel deposits in history. The new farm owner became instantly wealthy.

Sometimes there's more value in nickel than there is in gold if it's a large enough deposit. If you are a born-again child of God, there are valuable destiny deposits within you that need to be exposed and cultivated! Have you taken the time to discover what's been buried in your spirit since before the foundations of the world?

When you receive Christ there is inherent greatness in you that needs to be drawn out and activated for Kingdom growth and harvest. That's what we did at our ministry—after we realized the God-given value within us, we drew out our ministry identity and pattern and called it our own. We stopped trying to copy others and stepped into spiritual self-discovery. What we drew out through the process was uniquely us—our own God-given ministry identity and pattern. We have an inherent passion for it. We relate to it personally. We're not worn out trying to do something that was never us in the first place. We're excited and feel an electricity that lights us up. We have endless grace and energy serving in ministry. I no longer just "endure" ministry, I "enjoy" it—ministry is life-giving!

Within our team-up leadership structure we determined certain characteristics that described who we are and what we valued. Doing ministry now emanates from our being which in turn validates and fulfills us. I no longer serve another man's passion. I no longer speak with another man's voice. I speak that which God has verbalized in *my* spirit. The subconscious desire of my spirit that has guided me in the past has now been recognized and defined.

That is my full time job now. I help leaders discover their hidden deposits. Then I help them help others discover their hidden deposits. It's like the movie "War of Worlds"—the aliens had planted machines in the earth millions of years earlier and when modern-day spaceships came, they drew them out of the ground and activated them.

I now speak from what God has put within me. There's no greater integrity than being true to your God-given identity. There was always a subtle feeling of dishonesty whenever I tried to do ministry that wasn't truly me. Core values cannot be violated in our search for success without consequence. Our need for significance and self-worth can mislead us. It can mislead us when we see the success of someone else and then we copy him or her in an effort to copy his or her success. Even if we have some success, we damaged our personal sense of passion placed in us by God if we seek after another man's gold. Like the farmer in New England, it's not our deep deposit of nickel.

I'm sorry to say that I see this scenario frequently in ministry. Pastors who have planted what appear to be successful churches tell me that they're not happy with what they've accomplished. They say that if they weren't being paid to be the pastor there, they wouldn't attend their own church. What they've done is not consistent with what is in their heart. They don't even want to be with the people that they're pastoring.

I experienced the same thing after about 15 years in ministry. I didn't like what was produced in the church. My own need for significance misguided me. I realized that I was more of a success monger than a shepherd who was following the Great Shepherd. I had built a ministry that made me want to quit the ministry because I knew in my heart that something very serious was missing.

Success isn't just getting what you want—it's wanting it after you get it. Serving the Lord is the same common thread holding pastors and leaders together; but using the unique pattern that He created in us to serve Him brings ultimate fulfillment.

CHAPTER 8

SUCCESSFUL RETOOLING METHODS

After years of retooling my own ministry and many others across the United States, I have identified the following ministry pattern characteristics that bring success:

1. *High Standard of Excellence* – Quality music, helps ministry, teaching, instruction, facility maintenance, correspondence and publications, multimedia and brochures, presentation. Personal appearance of ministry staff is neat, clean, and polished.

2. *Equal Opportunity* – Male, female, race, age, and nationality—everyone must meet standards of excellence equally, no exceptions.

3. *Honor People* – Be punctual. Deliver what you promise. Build-up, don't beat-up. Honor time frames and appointments.

4. *Preach the Word* – Handle the Word of God with the highest regard. No liberties taken with interpretation.

5. *Spirit-filled* – Baptized in the Holy Spirit with the evidence of speaking in tongues. The gifts are free to operate.

6. *Worship* – Praise and worship is a vital part of every service. The prophetic song of the Lord and flow is important. Music ministry excellence.

7. *Prayer* – In every service and small group. Prayer for individual needs and corporate.

8. *Small Group Ministry* – Everyone involved in small groups receiving pastoral care, discipleship, and leadership development. Relationships are important and are built in small groups. Community is experienced.

9. *Importance of the Local Church* – People need to be connected to the local church. Small group ministry is aimed at connecting people to God, each other, and their local church. The small group is not the local church. The local church unites small groups to fulfill the great commission. The local church is the mailbox for every believer. God gives His blessing, protection, and covering in the local church.

10. *Apostolic Ministry* – Interchurch and regional ministry of the five-fold lineage is important. An apostolic leader and senior elder leads and projects the vision of the house. He is connected and submitted to other apostolic leaders and unites the churches to impact the region and initiates our mission thrust. He leads the top-level leaders and leads the structure development of the other churches. Other apostolic leaders can specialize and minister within the church.

11. *Discipleship* – We value Christ-likeness. Every believer must become a disciple of growth and change into Christ-likeness.

12. *Investing* – Tithing and giving offerings to the local church. Investing time in relationships with those who lead us and those we lead in the family and in the church. Invest in others including mentors and life coaches.

13. *Family Values* – Marriage and family are important. Ministry aimed at restoring marriages, families, and those who have suffered through divorce. Physical intimacy is sanctified only within the bonds of marriage. The homosexual lifestyle is damaging to the individual and the family.

14. *Drama and Arts* – Use all means available to present the gospel.

15. *Fruitfulness* – Produce the character fruit of Jesus Christ in the life of every Christian. The Bible speaks of the fruit of the Spirit—there is fruitfulness of ministry that brings numerical increase to the Body of Christ. "...*the Lord added to the church daily...*" (see Acts 2:47).

16. *Great Commission* – Every believer is involved in reaching the lost for Christ. Conduct joint annual missions' conferences to raise awareness and increase support and involvement for church planting and missions' mobilization both locally, regionally, nationally, and internationally.

IMPLEMENTATION

After determining our core values and pattern of ministry we went on to develop a process for implementing our pattern of ministry. Beyond our team-up leadership structure we needed a process for "people development." With our leadership teams in place, our core values defined, and our ministry pattern identified, we moved forward toward implementation and multiplication.

During this time of ministry transition, I had a prophetic dream. I dreamed that I was on board a ship heading out to sea and everything in the dream was in black, white, and gray. It was stormy and depressing as we sailed. The plumbing was backed up and the entire crew was depressed and stressed out. It was a horrible journey. Then the ship reached its final destination and we exited the ship while it was still storming and raining. We walked up a very steep embankment and wondered if we would ever reach the top. Then all of a sudden the storm disappeared and everything burst into color. The sky was blue, the sun was shining, and all around us were trees laden with fruit. Then the Lord spoke audibly and said to me, "You've seen what man can do with missions, now I'm going to show you what I can do."

I believe in interpreting that dream that the Lord was challenging me to focus on ships—fellowship, relationship, discipleship, leadership, craftsmanship, and stewardship. The backed-up plumbing in the dream represented the need for function systems. We need systems and processes for people development in the Church.

At the time, our ministry was totally event-oriented and was suffering from the lack of process for growing up and transforming people. This lack also caused stress and overload because of the top-heavy burden of counseling and pastoral care of the congregation. For years since that dream I've devoted my studies to these important "ships" and together with the leadership team we developed a process of people development using these ships.

God can do a lot in people through "shipbuilding." Our process of people development begins with reaching new people in our area of influence through *fellowship* opportunities at the church or in small groups. All the scheduled events we plan are strategically designed to bring people on board by recruiting them from the event into a small group.

SHIP LEVELS

We developed a six-level implementation program for people development:

Level One—Fellowship

Level Two—Relationship

Level Three—Discipleship

Level Four—Leadership

Level Five—Craftsmanship

Level Six—Stewardship

Our goal is to bring people through each level until they reach their full potential at Level Six—leader of their own ministry.

Level One—Fellowship. Invite people in the community to come to a small group or event. Unsaved family, friends, and coworkers don't usually relate to the typical charismatic church service. (It may even frighten them because they don't understand what's going on.) We use fellowship opportunities to bridge the gap between being unchurched to attending a service. Newcomers learn how to play a guitar, knit, take a hunter safety course, play volleyball, etc.

After they get to know us in an event or small group environment, they become open and less fearful when they attend church services. We have a very strong core value for our Pentecostal charismatic roots. We're not willing to compromise. At the same time, we're not willing to compromise the mandate to reach the lost. We get to meet and greet people in fellowship groups and events.

Level Two—Relationship. Level Two events and small groups focus on relationship building. People learn how to master forgiveness, and build a better relationship with Christ, themselves, and others.

Connecting with people relationally will attract involvement. We value relationships in our ministry. We value people and bring them on board by appealing to their need to develop healthy relationships. The average person in the United States is very much alone. Studies show that people only have two close relationships with others. That number is down from three close relationships just ten years ago. The drop may be a result of people being eaten up with the "please disease" and have been hurt relationally. Therefore they isolate themselves to avoid being hurt again.

Most folks today are relationally fearful and lonely. First, we have to get our own house healthy, and then we can bring others on board and lead them into relational health. Prospective leaders are encouraged to attend Level Two small groups and overcome their relational hurts and dysfunctions during their team-up leadership training.

The leader of a small group shares his or her testimony or has a conversational prayer time that lasts about ten minutes each time they meet together. Other events can include a woman's luncheon, mother-daughter tea, father-son campout, Mother's Day, Father's Day, or holiday events. Then visitors can be invited to attend a small group that centers on issues related to those topics.

Level Three—Discipleship. Discipleship connects people to God, themselves, and each other. There is a great need for discipleship in our culture because sharing the gospel is only the first step to building the Kingdom of God. Many problems the average Christian experiences are the result of their lack of discipleship. They haven't mastered themselves under the Master. Christ-likeness can only take place through the process of effective discipleship.

Small groups are where we roll up our sleeves and work on developing Christ-likeness. We invite people into our lives to help us become the person He designed us to be—someone we can love and admire. These small groups focus on developing the daily disciplines of prayer, devotions, Bible reading, and study. Nothing predicts a person's future more than their daily routine. Just ask a professional golfer about the importance of their routine.

The goal is for people to be transformed not just educated. I use a little story to illustrate the evangelistic affect of transformation. This is actually a joke that I heard and made some modifications: A young Amish boy turned 13 years old and wanted to visit the outside world. He convinced his dad to take the family to the local shopping mall to see what it was like there.

As they walked through the mall the young boy was quite wide-eyed. One thing in particular caught his eye—two metal doors that slid open and closed by themselves. Above the doors were small round numbers that would light up. People would walk through the doors and disappear and others would appear and walk out.

The boy brought his father to show him what he'd found. "Dad," he asked pointing to the elevator, "what is that?" At that very moment an elderly lady pushing a walker in front of her rolled up to the doors of the elevator. When the doors opened, she walked in and the doors closed behind her. As the boy and his father watched, a few moments later the doors opened and out walked a beautiful, blond, 20-year-old young lady. Dad was astonished—"Quick! Go get your Mama, son!"

Transformation gets people's attention. There's no better method of evangelism than a changed life. Lives don't change by attending events—it takes a process of discipleship to fully transform lives from darkness into light. Events are good entry points for people to begin the process of transformation, though.

We schedule events at the end of a small group series where people can make important commitments after they finish a course or teaching series like "Cleansing Streams" or "Inner Healing." Jesus took His disciples through a journey of discipleship transformation that ultimately changed the world they lived in. Others could see that though they were merely fishermen and ordinary men, because they had been with Jesus they had been transformed.

Discipleship is not rulership. Some movements in the '70s tried that tactic and made a big mess in people's lives.

Level Four—Leadership. First we want people to experience community and fellowship. Then we want them to be healed and learn to build healthy relationships with themselves and others before they start leading others. At Level Four, leaders emerge. The first aspect of effective healthy leadership is self-leadership. After people experience transformation in their own lives and relationships, they want others to experience it too.

After people become disciples they must move on to the final stage of discipleship—making disciples. Becoming a leader means sharing with others the benefits of their own discipleship and enrolling others into that process as mentors and life coaches. Small groups are where we practice leadership as well as learn the art of servant leadership. Training events also equip and empower leaders for more effective service.

Level Five—Craftsmanship. This level involves top-level leaders of leaders who have their own ministry. Their ministry focuses on empowering their leaders and the leaders they lead for effective ministry. Craftsmen learn how to build a ministry and to coach and mentor others to do the same by following their pattern of ministry. At this level they learn the importance of developing systems, processes, and structures that help others build their own ministries. Small group seminars, workshops, and training events help leaders hone their ministry skills.

Level Six—Stewardship. Leadership is being good stewards of the leaders God has given us. We do that by taking responsibility to make sure our leaders are being sufficiently challenged and trained. We meet in small groups to overview the ministry to be sure we are offering a balanced menu of levels. We must be sure that there are groups and events available for all levels of the people development process; and that we're continually offering our leaders opportunities to move them forward toward their goal. Regional events are planned with top-level leaders that offer specialization training. We also work together regionally for missions mobilization and train potential candidates for church plants and missionary programs. Pastors and apostolic leaders work together in teams of six to assure the stewardship of our leadership.

Establishing these six levels of people development gave our leadership something they could buy into. This structure allowed them to direct potential leaders through a clear track starting at Level Three as a disciple and assistant group leader. They could reproduce leaders through a defined process. As mentioned previously, you can't reproduce something until you define it.

JOINING THE TEAM

When prospective members ask us about becoming a part of our ministry we can now offer them an inspirational and exciting path for involvement. We offer them the opportunity to become members, lead a small group, or follow the leadership development track toward full-time ministry.

Because we have determined our ministry identity, defined our core values, and implemented our unique ministry pattern, we can meet the needs of our members and potential members like never before.

The following are a few steps that we share with potential members so they know what to expect. We emphasize that these steps will not only enhance their local church experience but will grow their relationship with their heavenly Father.

STEPS TO FULFILLING YOUR GOD-GIVEN POTENTIAL:

1. *Fellowship—Attend regularly.* Have fellowship with us on a regular basis. Attend Sunday services and small group events.

We welcome you to become involved in our many activities developed to provide fellowship for you and your family.

2. *Relationship*—Become a member and attend a small group. Build relationships and friendships by faithfully attending church services and a small group. It takes time to develop relationships and we look forward to moving beyond knowing you as a casual acquaintance to knowing you as part of our family of God.

3. *Discipleship*—Become a disciple by learning to be led, and assist leading a small group.

4. *Leadership*—Lead a small group and develop an assistant leader. Disciple others as a "disciple maker" by leading a small group.

5. *Craftsmanship*—Lead a group of leaders. Learn how to build a ministry team of leaders who lead small groups.

6. *Multiplication*—The key to unlocking the end-time harvest. Help develop excellence in ministry in yourself and others, and multiply teams churchwide.

After my "ship" dream, I have since learned that the word *apostle* was used to describe leaders from the Roman Empire who were sent out to establish a new colony as an extension of Rome. An apostle actually led a fleet of ships that sailed until they found a place suitable for a colony. When they found a location, they built a colony that looked much like Rome. They lived by the Roman culture and law and made the new-found colony an expansion of the Roman Empire.

Today's apostolic leader does the same thing by leading a fleet of ships (churches) to colonize new regions for Kingdom expansion.

CHAPTER 9

TEAM VISION AND GOALS

Before the retooling of our ministry, I used to go away and pray and ask God for direction and guidance concerning what our vision should be and what goals we should set as a ministry to accomplish them. Then I would write down what was in my heart and set goals for each area of ministry.

When I returned, I made a copy for each of the pastoral staff and then I told them who we are and what we were going to do. I spoke, they agreed, and that was about as far as it would go for the year. It was my vision and my goals for each one of them to accomplish. The only action that really took place concerning fulfilling the vision and goals was their patronizing reaction. They seemed impressed—but it wasn't *our* vision and *our* goals. It was *my* vision and goals that I had given to them and called it ours. I think they forgot the vision before the meeting even adjourned! Now I know the value of including every member of our pastoral team when it comes to developing our ministry's vision and setting ministry goals.

The staff hadn't caught my passion because they weren't there when I was going through the process that birthed the vision and set the goals. Back then, I was just doing what I was taught as a top-down leader. All the leaders in the church agreed that this was the way the anointed man of God was supposed lead. I was Moses going to the "mountaintop," to receive the vision from God. Then I was to tell everyone what God told me to tell them. At that time I never thought about including them in the "mountaintop" process and experience.

As a result, we were plagued for years with a lack of ownership when it came to the vision and the goals for carrying it out. The leaders almost cringed when I gave them their annual goals. Before long, goals were laid aside because we were tired and embarrassed about not accomplishing them. Vision was the topic I spoke on every first week in January. It was the time of the year when I introduced a new theme like "Power from Heaven in '97." Vision, or the lack of it, did not drive every decision and dictate how every dollar was spent—like it does now.

In reality, back then we had several different visions happening in the church that at times turned into di-vision. *Division* is defined as "more than one vision." Division can only happen when one vision is not adequately broadcasted throughout the church—and when there is no buy in by the leadership.

First we had to get on the right broadcast station when it came to vision. We had to get on what I call the "**WIIFM**" station. I had learned that people don't hear what we're saying until they hear "**W**hat's **I**n **I**t **F**or **M**e." Unless pastoral staff and key leadership members are included in the process and buy into the vision, there will be no vision—no goals accomplished. When there is buy in at the top levels, they will in turn include their secondary team members in the vision process and so on throughout the ministry until everyone involved becomes vision owners.

My dilemma: how to include the other team members without giving away the pastor's God-given right and responsibility to lead. I feared that including others in vision development would somehow dilute or take away from my right to lead them where God was leading me. My concern was based on the possibility that our ministry would turn into a democratic consensus-driven ministry. I had seen how voting had caused a lot of political upheaval in churches and slowed progress to a crawl. I didn't want that to happen.

If there is a vote for every decision, it isn't long before we're making decisions based on political payback instead of decisions that lead to progress. In that scenario, "God-called leadership" wouldn't have much of a voice, resulting in a loss of theologically led leadership. This had been my experience in both the Baptist and Assembly of God churches that I had attended before entering the pastoral ministry. Consensus-driven leadership to me was so obviously obstructive to effective leadership that I chose to serve the Lord in an independent charismatic church where I had the right to lead. Years later after having the right to make decisions, I could now see that it had produced a lack of buy in and kept people from owning the vision of the house and making it theirs.

Having the right to make decisions and lead others doesn't mean that others will automatically follow us. John Maxwell notes that if the pastor is leading and the leaders aren't following, the pastor's just taking a walk.[1] When it comes to vision and goal setting I realized that I had been "just taking a walk." I wasn't on the right frequency with our leaders until I answered the "what's in it for me" question.

Before I could invite the staff members to participate in the vision and goal process I had to define how our team would function and operate. That included clarifying my role as the team leader and their roles as team members. We had to agree how we would make decisions as a team. Everyone understood that the team leader needed to be a Holy Spirit-called and led leader who would be accountable to God for making the right decisions. We also agreed that final decisions would be made, in most cases, only after we had gone through the process of team dialogue, ideological conflict, and interaction.

As the team leader, I had the right to make the final decisions within the obvious boundaries of Scripture. After we defined our team leadership roles we became more effective as a team in developing our entire leadership infrastructure. Because I made the final decisions, we were able to avoid the pitfalls of being consensus driven. The other team members had a say in the decision making process which created buy in from everyone on the team. Team members bought into the process not because we always did what they wanted, but because their opinions were heard and influenced the decisions *before* they were made. We were no longer a one-person, top-down structure, and we didn't turn into a mob-rule, democratic leadership. Our new team ministry model met in the middle between the two extremes of top-down and consensus-driven leadership.

LOCALLY, REGIONALLY, GLOBALLY

Needless to say this transition revolutionized our ministry. Now when we developed the vision I included the team and got their fingerprints on the blueprints. I became more like a facilitator, and instead of telling the leaders my vision I asked the team questions that provoked them to think and become engaged in the process. In answering the questions, we fleshed out from within us what became the vision of the house. It was amazing how the vision emerged as each individual person shared their hearts.

As a result, the leaders became vision owners. During the actual discussion process, we wrote down what we valued and how we've been led in terms of doing ministry in the past and present. Our vision statement was the culmination and condensation of all of our hearts and it just popped out of the mouth of one of the leaders. I couldn't have said it better myself. It was the first time we had a vision statement that didn't come word for word out of my, the pastor's, mouth. Someone heard our hearts' cry and summarized it as the process came to a boil. The leader didn't stay with us for the long haul but he made a lasting contribution.

Our vision statement: "Growing together locally, reaching out regionally, and sending forth globally."

Everyone in all four of our churches—Churches in the Lead—can tell you our vision. It dictates every decision made and every dollar spent. It can be seen in the agenda of every program and heard in every prayer meeting.

We carry out our vision *locally* through events and small groups that are strategically designed to reach the lost, make disciples, and develop reproducing leaders.

We carry out our vision *regionally* through specialized training events and classes for all areas of ministry. Together we host regional training for just about every area of ministry including men, women, children, youth, singles, music, audio/video communications, small group and leadership training, marriage, healing and deliverance, prophet schools, pastoral and ministry development, domestic and foreign mission awareness, and more.

We carry out our vision of sending forth *globally* by raising support for missions and church planting in each of our churches. Together we unite in our world mission efforts—financially and strategically—so that act as one ministry reaching the world. We host mission trips to foreign countries giving all our church members a great commission experience. The pastor in each church goes on at least one mission trip a year.

As the apostolic leader of Churches in the Lead, it is my responsibility to take the lead in developing a world harvest mission strategy. It is also my privilege to lead the regional apostolic mission team comprised of pastors (one from each of our churches). Together we decide who we will support, what churches we will plant, and who we will recognize and develop from within Churches in the Lead as our next potential ministry candidates for full time staff ministry, church plant pastors, traveling ministry, and missionaries. We also develop strategies for communicating the vision and importance that every church be "mission minded" and "world harvest focused."

As an apostolic leader I am also training the pastors on my team to lead a future apostolic team as the need arises through church multiplication. At our current rate of growth we will need another apostolic team leader in the next few years. Each apostolic team leader leads a team of up to six pastors along with their churches. When we grow to six churches, we will plant the next six churches under the leadership of one of the pastors on my team who is ready to transition into the apostolic. Our vision would continue to unfold with the goal of developing each pastor on the team who had the desire and potential to transition into the apostolic to do so. Teams of pastors would become teams of apostolic leaders who each led six pastors as the down-lines of leadership and churches multiply.

Our vision for Churches in the Lead is to multiply our churches starting with one church that is being led by one pastor who has transitioned into the apostolic as a leader. Most church planters historically remain pastors and never make the transition into regional leadership. They just keep adding churches and never move into the multiplication aspect of leadership. Having to start over several times without inherent people and resources to build upon ultimately depletes the church planter personally and severely taxes their family.

The church they leave behind seldom makes a connection or catches the vision for Kingdom advancement and more often they feel abandoned when the founder and church planter leaves. If a totally different leader takes over, the congregation can feel disillusioned or disenfranchised. The new pastor may not always follow the same vision and share the same core values as the planting pastor. A multiplication ministry strategy allows the planting pastor to remain the overseeing leader who replaces himself with a spiritual son or daughter who in turn has the same vision and core values. A DNA match greatly increases the chances that the new church will continue to grow and maintain its identity integrity and then participate in supporting future church plants continuing the Kingdom expansion.

The next multiplication would be 36 churches being led by six apostles. The next would multiply to 216 churches being led by an additional 36 apostles. Ultimately the vision is unlimited in its potential for leadership multiplication. It would take about 11 down-line team multiplications to assimilate the world's population. As a matter of fact, that's exactly how the world was populated in the first place. Families (teams) simply multiplied beginning with Adam and Eve and the rest is history.

MULTIPLICATION

Just like a healthy family, the benefits of developing regional teams are numerous. Every pastor would have a pastor who, as an apostolic leader, would provide them leadership and pastoral care. Each pastor would also belong to a community of other pastors that they could fellowship with and learn from. The apostle would act as the lead journey taker, providing spiritual leadership and on-going mentoring with the pastors. Effective team ministry has the potential to eliminate the isolation and loneliness that has such a negative impact on today's pastors and their families. Pastors would also have somewhere to grow and go next.

The apostolic multiplication of churches is another church growth option in addition to the megachurch option. There are multiple churches under one ministry umbrella led by an apostolic leader who has transitioned from a pastor leading one church to the apostolic ministry of leading multiple churches. The apostolic leader, in effect, pastors and leads a region. When that apostolic leader reproduces other apostolic leaders, it results in regional expansion and regional multiplication.

Some areas of the country are not as spiritually fertile as others when it comes to building large congregations. As a result, most pastors never experience congregational growth beyond 200 members. They don't want to leave where they are and start all over again with little to no resources. So they just plateau and maintain.

Like my experience, pastors may keep trying to break the 200 barrier and get discouraged. I finally realized that if I couldn't get any higher, I'd go wider. If you have faith for a 100- or 200-member church, then do what you know you can do—again. Repeat what you've already had faith for and do it multiple times. Multiple church ministries helped me to hone my leadership skills for doing greater works on a larger scale.

We have now grown to four churches with the goal of starting at least one new church per year. Attendance at each of our four churches averages about 150-200 people. After we grow to a total of six churches, a second apostolic leader will be raised up to lead the next six new churches. Each apostolic team will then look to plant at least one church per year. Apostolic team multiplication will result in doubling or multiplying new church plants.

Up until the time we initiated the multiplication expansion model, our ministry offered no future for pastors who had reached their limit of 200-or-less member churches. There was no incentive for them to keep going and growing. In most denominational churches pastors climb the career ladder by leaving a small-member church for a bigger one. It can more often lead to Kingdom competition instead of Kingdom expansion. Our vision offers pastors an endless opportunity for leadership and church multiplication.

SETTING GOALS

After the vision is established, we move forward setting goals for carrying out the mission. It is critical to include those who will be involved in carrying out the goals when we set the goals. Like with the vision, the leadership needs to take ownership of the goals to guarantee a successful outcome.

The pastor, as the team leader, leads each staff member to develop initial goals representing every area of ministry in the church. Everyone's goals must be consistent with the house core values and pattern. Every goal is then brought down-line where the staff member (who serves as a team leader with the pastor) now becomes the team leader to six other leaders. As the team leader, that person now includes the other leaders for goal setting for their specific areas of ministry.

Involving leaders from the top-level team throughout the remaining ministry teams, assures leader and team buy in for accomplishing the goals.

I learned an exercise from my pastor, Steven Vickers, that I use to engage the members of my team in the vision process. I started using this vision exercise as a pastor, and now I've expanded it to all levels of ministry. The following few paragraphs explain the exercise.

The pastor, as the team leader, gathers together the other team members (who are top-level leaders in all the various areas of ministry in the church). Then pastor says something like, "Let's imagine that we just had the best church service in the history of this church. Everything that could go right did go right. Everyone was firing on all cylinders and we were all working together like never before. Now that being the case, describe it to me. Exactly what would that scenario look like to you?"

The leader facilitates the meeting discussion and helps keep the sequence of events in proper order. For instance, the conversation should begin describing the pre-service prayer or service preparation rather than the music or a portion of the service that comes toward the end. The leader can redirect the discussion by asking something such as, "Is that where the Sunday church service actually begins? We need to talk about the entire process of the 'best service ever.'"

Next, everyone contributes their vision about the "best service ever." The pastor (team leader) needs to make sure they understand that there are no right or wrong answers during this exercise. The leader's goal is to draw out every team member's individual responses and write them on a large chalk or white board in the room where everyone can see them.

Together they sequentially move through and describe every aspect of the Sunday church service. This exercise "takes them" there instead of "telling them" there. This exercise brings each one of them into the process of vision development. You can't buy it if you can't see it. I had to quit telling people what I saw and start empowering them to see it for themselves.

The vision doesn't become theirs until it comes out of their heart and is spoken out of their mouth. Until that takes place, there will never be team vision ownership. A wise leader learns how to ask the right questions. I had to learn to ask people questions, knowing that the answers to the questions I asked them would become the vehicle taking them to where we were going. They might get there a different way than I would take, but that was fine with me. I was learning how to be a "vision sharer" instead of a "vision dominator." Through this exercise we learned that God was speaking through each one of us as we participated in the vision process. To my delight the team members actually voiced a lot more detail than I would have if I had written the description myself.

As a result of going through this vision process together we defined every aspect of the Sunday morning worship service. Until we took this vision journey together we all had different expectations of what needed to take place. Also, we were only focused on what we did personally in ministry as opposed to what we did together as a team. Now we all had the same vision of what ministry was supposed to look and act like.

Then we agreed to apply the vision development process to each area of ministry within the church. As a team we talked about each team member's area or department of ministry. After input about what each ministry would look like, each team member took the vision list to the leaders on their team down-line. They repeated the discussion process and asked them the questions that would bring their leaders vision buy in.

For example, the children's ministry team leader (who is also a team member on the executive leadership team led by the pastor) met with her team and repeated the vision process with the children ministry team. The children ministry team had up to six team members who led various departments such as the nursery, toddlers, preschool, children's church, or small groups for children. The team leader had prepared questions that gave the other team members the opportunity to be part of vision development. The answers to those questions became the vision and goals of the children's ministry team.

An action plan for accomplishing the goals determined what the children's ministry would do in terms of curriculum choice and program development. They also set goals for recruiting and training leaders and servants. They owned the thinking and planning to have the greatest children's ministry our church has ever had.

This new way of implementing our vision and accomplishing our goals rejuvenated and empowered the staff. No longer did ministry team leaders have to wait on the pastor to tell them what to do next or to catch what might be missing or need to be repaired.

Annually, the pastor and the executive leadership team overviews each ministry's vision, goals, and action plan to ensure that each area of ministry has goals that are consistent with the ministry's core values, house DNA, pattern, and doctrine. Goals are also reviewed to ensure they are comprehensive and meet the needs and fulfill the vision of the house for that area of ministry. It must be clear that each ministry hasn't become "the" ministry but that each serves together with other ministries to the betterment of a whole and healthy ministry.

At times, goals are tweaked as they advance through the higher levels of the leadership team structure. Final approval is given at the pastor's team level. The team leader has the final say on decisions made by their team. Every team leader also serves as a team member on the next higher level team and the team leader at that level has the final say in decision making.

MAINTENANCE

After the vision and action plan are in place, the executive leadership team makes everyone on their team accountable by monitoring progress and coaching throughout the year. Each executive team member assumes the team leader role in their down-line team and together they repeat the process in each of their down-line teams.

We began with one team that included me as the pastor and six staff members. As the team leader, I helped them become secondary team leaders. Their job in the secondary team was to reproduce after the model of our team. They recruited and trained others who after time became team leaders on a third level.

Before long, several of my team members actually grew to become pastors of their own churches, and we had to develop a higher level regional apostolic executive team. My role at that point changed in response to the leadership needs of our pastors and churches. I became the apostolic leader of Churches in the Lead. By then, our teams had actually expanded up and down!

Now we were in new territory and had to retool our leadership roles and structures. Now I had to lead the fleet—as well as train the pastors to lead their ships. The pastors led their teams to grow and reproduce teams that resulted in multiplying lay ministry leaders in each of their churches. The pastor has the final say in the local church subject to the apostolic team leader. The apostolic team leader has the final say, subject to the apostolic board of directors.

This leadership and multiplication structure has been a great success in bringing glory to His Kingdom. Goals and decisions are made by all team members, no matter the level. All team members have the opportunity to influence the decisions leaders make instead of making decisions for them. Ministry success is the goal of all; therefore all must be involved in important ministry decisions. Empowerment throughout the leadership structure means a healthy and successful ministry.

The authority of the team leader is beneficial. Serving and leading others becomes our role as executive servant leaders. As mentioned previously, correction is best received when it comes from a peer level. However, the team leader will correct a team member if peers are fearful or unwilling.

SETTING REGIONAL MINISTRY GOALS

Regional ministry goals are set much the same way as those within the church. Each pastor on the apostolic team serves as the down-line team leader for different regional events. Each apostolic team member leads a team where his gifts can be most helpful.

For example, one of our pastors had previously served successfully as a youth pastor. He is gifted in youth ministry more than the other members on the apostolic team so he leads the youth ministry team (one from each church). The apostolic team members list criteria concerning regional youth rally events and leadership training. He meets with all the youth pastors and together they set goals and plan events to carry out those goals for the region. The apostolic team gives the final approval and they proceed.

Another member of our apostolic team leads the regional music ministry team because he was formerly a music minister. Together with a team that includes a music minister from each of our four churches they set goals for regional music training events as well as for supporting the music needs for regional conferences and seminars.

Another member of our team leads the regional intercessory prayer ministry. That person set goals for regional training events as well as for supporting the region in prayer coverage. We chose this woman because she has a gifting in intercession.

Another team member leads the prophetic regional team because the person is prophetically gifted. We identified and installed a champion with certain specializations of ministry with the purpose of improving and expanding their impact on our entire region.

Regional goals are set for every area of specialization by teams led by a different member of the apostolic team. By including the top-level leaders from each church in the regional goal setting, planning, and implementation process, there is a very high level of buy in and participation from every church.

Each ministry leader returns to their local church and gets their team on board for the regional events (that they helped plan) for the benefit of their own local church. When the leaders of the local church ministries are involved in the planning and carrying out of ministry training events we are assured that they know what their leaders need the most. And if they don't know, we can ask them the questions that will reveal those needs.

I learned the importance of buy in when I tried to pastor three churches from the top-down. It was physically possible for me to attend two services on Sunday morning and exert my leadership influence to generate participation in regional events and activities. But the shoes started to fall, however, when we grew to three churches. Many events were poorly attended because I just couldn't master that "omnipresence" thing Sunday mornings especially when the services were 30 minutes apart. It was then when I realized I had to extend my influence through others.

REDEFINING ROLES

Leadership multiplication through others is the closest thing to being omnipresent. God tricked me when the third church came along. Before the church became a part of our ministry, I had been the overseer of the third church's pastor and served on their board of directors. When their pastor resigned, I took the church under our wing and made them a part of our ministry family. Until then I was pastoring two churches successfully. The new church was an hour away from the home church, though, unlike the second church which was only 30 minutes away. That extra traveling time was just a little too much of a stretch for me to fit into a Sunday morning!

I was beginning to think that God was taking advantage of me. I thought at the time "Well that's all I need, another church." Was God having a hard time getting help? Doesn't God know that I need time to pray and study and maybe rest once in a while? I just couldn't fit three churches into my existing paradigm.

I actually started looking for a pastor who I could turn the church over to. In the meantime, my wife actually volunteered to help me pastor the new church. She acted as the interim pastor while I searched for a new pastor. I called all over the country to no avail. It didn't seem like anyone I knew wanted to move to New England where it's cold and has about a 20 percent higher cost of living. My wife worked together with me just like the other ministers on staff in our other two churches. She did an outstanding job and ended up becoming the permanent pastor. This is now our fastest growing church.

I was unknowingly being maneuvered and transitioned by the Holy Spirit into apostolic ministry. But all that I knew and identified within ministry was in the context of me being pastoral. I had invited Prophet Ed Traut to come to our churches and when he did, he prophesied to me that I was making a transition into the apostolic. He also prophesied that another person (one of my spiritual sons) would become the pastor in the home church. He said that I would be the father but another would be the pastor.

When we concluded the church service that day I invited Ed back to our house for some food and fellowship. He didn't waste any time. He asked me, "So Ron, what's your vision?" I told him my vision and he said, "No, I'm not asking you about your vision as a pastor. I'm asking about your vision as an apostle." At first it aggravated me that he would ask me a question that I didn't have an answer for. I thought, *Gee, this guy doesn't even know me and already he's trying to embarrass me?*

In actuality, he was challenging me and requiring me to stop leading like a pastor and start leading like an apostle. Through him, God was speaking loud and clear to me about thinking and seeing in terms of a multiple church ministry. I had instead been trying to lead an apostolic ministry with a pastoral mind and skill set. Being a pastor was all I knew then and even that was changing fast. My frustrations in ministry at that time were caused by the limitations of my pastoral gifting. I would have to learn how to lead in a whole new way now.

In some ways it felt like I was disconnecting from the home church or in some way losing them. I feared that ministering and leading through others could somehow make me less needed or appreciated by the people in our churches. My identity needs were met by serving as the pastor. I was important in their eyes; and could see that every time I spoke to them from the pulpit.

Finding my identity in what I was doing was the very thing that kept me from changing what I was doing. It became the lid of my ministry. I've since learned that my identity is found in Christ. My identity is more about *being* than it is about *doing*. I am God's child. My value is determined by being a member of God's family. As a member of God's family I have family privileges and a family inheritance. Who I am, is more about *whose* I am. What God had for me next was what God was doing in me.

As a pastor I determined my value and identity through the eyes of others. But my true spiritual identity can only be seen through the eyes of my heavenly Father. If we're defined only by what we do then we'll never do anything new. Our new identity is held back by the existing identity. For the born-again Christian old things are passing away while all things are becoming new. (See 2 Corinthians 5:17.) It's hard for things to pass away as long as you have made them a part of your identity. In one way, the prophet said things that made me excited about something new; and in another way, what he said threatened to turn the apple cart over in terms of how I saw myself serving in ministry.

In reality, my life wasn't about to change, it was already changing. And I was just now facing it. All the things I had been doing in an effort to lead and manage the ministry of two churches were not just things I did to try to cope with the demands of multiple church ministry. The apostolic gifting was in operation and I was the only one who hadn't completely faced it yet. It was a set up from the Lord! I've since told people that God tricked me by leading me into a ministry transition before I knew what was happening. Some of the limitations and challenges that frustrated me were no longer relevant when I quit facing them as a "pastor." Now that I was facing it without those limitations I was free to make needed changes as an "apostle."

Prophet Ed Traut made me do some serious soul searching concerning who I was and what I was supposed to be doing. Within six months I had completely transitioned out of the role of pastor and into my new role as an apostolic team leader of pastors. Our pastors and leaders also started growing at a quickened pace in what seemed to be an apparent reaction to my transition.

As I shared with other pastors and leaders outside of our local ministry about what God was doing in our ministry, they were interested in learning more. Pastors from all over the country asked me to provide apostolic leadership for them and their churches. I agreed to serve, when asked, as National

Church Empowerment Director for our ministerial fellowship. In that role I served other pastors by helping them develop their vision and empower their leaders. This book is mainly a result of being asked to write it. Sharing our success is a privilege and a pleasure when it moves forward His Kingdom on earth as it is in Heaven.

Looking back now, I see that the trigger point for the ministry transformation was the prophetic word that changed how I saw myself.

Once we transitioned our regional ministry to function as an apostolic team, we had to change how we set our goals as well as how we accomplished them. I had to learn how to get our pastors involved and make them joint vision owners and show them how to get buy in from their team right on down through every ministry in each of their churches. We were all excited and in agreement that this was the leading of the Lord for all of us who have since became Churches in the Lead. Each pastor knows that they can someday do what I'm doing if that's what God has for them. Or they can be content to continue their current work.

Our team ministry process has been effective in producing and multiplying healthy leaders in both small churches and in megachurches. It has been proven fruitful in wounded churches as well as in healthy churches. We've planted new churches starting them with the team ministry from the very beginning. We have also seen our team process work well for business men and women. In implementing team-up principles in their business or on their job they found that they had more time for ministry involvement.

SETTING WORLD HARVEST GOALS

We realized after we transitioned into a regional ministry that our churches could work together and have an even greater impact. We were no longer an individual church with minimal resources. I used to tell everyone in our ministry what we were going to do for world missions and outreach and that's what we'd do. Now that I wasn't there in every pulpit and at every Sunday church service, something had to change concerning global outreach. Missions support and involvement actually declined for a time until I realized that I had to get the pastors on board with me first. And then by working together, we would have greater impact on world harvest.

The other pastors didn't all have the same passion, insight, or experience that I did when it came to being a "great commission" minister leading a "great commission church." They looked to me to do that for us. I had to empower them and invite them to come on board and make it a vision they could call their own. After all, how could they influence and lead the church somewhere that they themselves weren't going?

This was just one more area in ministry that needed to be retooled. I realized I had to re-extend my influence. It was only in transitioning from my role as pastor that I could actually see and define the boundaries of my former leadership influence. When finances decreased or ministry support weakened, I realized we had to regain that loss of influence through the pastors who were on my team. This introspection became a positive way of helping define the roles and influence of pastoral leadership. It also modeled to them how to deal with the same issues where influence had declined with members on their down-line teams.

Regional Apostolic Team. Our world harvest vision and goals were developed by our regional apostolic team. Then each pastor on that team went back and got their executive leadership teams on board and eventually the entire church body. The regional apostolic team developed the strategy and agenda. Then we determined how we would communicate the vision and encourage buy in for world missions from each of our churches. We were all blown away when we saw the difference it made when we came up with a real comprehensive missions ministry program and strategy. World missions became our ministry, not just the apostolic leaders' ministry.

Reproducing. We decided that our world missions program would have the same ministry pattern as our overall Churches in the Lead DNA. We have a strong conviction that all ministries we support be not just a production but a reproduction. We wouldn't just support existing missions ministries or raise up missionaries but we would support and raise up missionary-producing missionaries. We would plant church-planting churches.

That meant that we would not support and invest in any ministry that ended when their minister left or went on to be with the Lord. There had to be a successor or a ministry that could provide one. I agree with Dr. Lester Sumrall who said that, "there is no such thing as a success without a successor." Standing firm on that core value meant stopping support for single-generation missionaries or one-man shows. This was a difficult decision because some of those ministries were led by long-time, close, personal friends of mine.

Local Ministries. We also agreed that we would support local benevolent ministries that serve the poor in the communities of each of our churches. Ministries like the Salvation Army, Operation Blessing, food pantries, and homeless shelters. We partner with these ministries and refer people to these ministries for help. These ministries already have the processes and systems in place to help those in need. Being involved and supporting benevolent ministry is community outreach. We all wanted to reach our own community first.

Church Planting. We also have a passion for church planting. The greatest gift you can give a town or a city is a local church. We have a goal of planting one church a year. We recruit members from each of our Churches in the Lead churches to serve on the church planting team. We decide together who will be the next church-planting pastor candidate. We determine a budget and fund its start up completely.

After we develop a region of six churches, we will develop new regions of six churches. We haven't developed more than one region yet, but we clearly see that in our future. Our goal is to plant one new church in each regional ministry. New regions would multiply new church plants.

Development and Funding. We set a goal to develop and fund more regional ministry infrastructure to support both regional and world harvest ministry. We brought our individual church computer database information and communication systems up to the regional level. We also defined every aspect of regional ministry as well as the role of a regional apostolic team leader for the purpose of future regional ministry reproduction. We are also developing a regional marketing strategy for promoting Churches in the Lead in our region through direct mail and media.

ENDNOTE

1. John C. Maxwell, *Developing the Leader Within You* (Nashville, TN: Thomas Nelson, 1993).

CHAPTER 10

PLANNING TEAM ACTION

The next step in the retooling process is developing an Action Plan or Annual Calendar. What good are goals if we don't commit to acting on them? Goals need to have specific actions planned and executed to be successfully accomplished.

ACTION PLAN CALENDAR

First we generally decide what *regional events and specialized training* we need to schedule for the next 1-3 years. Then we write in the dates for these planned activities on a large calendar. At this point we look at an overall schedule of events with more specific planning coming later in the process. We use an 18-month calendar because some regional training and ministry events are not necessary every year. Some regional events have to be planned three years ahead because of guest speakers' schedules.

We also plan our small group calendar three years in advance, reflecting the overall beginning and ending of small group semesters. Specific small group events are planned at the end of a current semester for the next semester. Guest ministries are invited during the break weeks of small groups so that we don't interrupt the momentum of our small groups. Guest ministries can be invited on Sunday mornings during the semesters because they don't make people choose between attending their small group and attending an extra church service or services.

After the regional events are planned we plan each *local church's calendar of events*. The pastor meets with each member of his or her executive team and they discuss their goals and plans for the future. They schedule on their master church calendar all the events that will help them meet their objectives. The pastor makes sure that everyone works together in the planning process, acting as the traffic director.

After the first calendar drafts (regional and local) are finished, they are scrutinized and screened by their respective teams. It is important for the entire team to buy into the calendar of events. We ask the following questions in our calendar of events screening process:

Are we balanced? Are we doing too much for some ministries and not enough for others? Depending on the team answers, some events are added and some activities are deleted. Are all of the "ships" represented? Do we have a ministry balance in terms of events designed for fellowship, relationship, discipleship, leadership, craftsmanship, and stewardship of leadership? Does our annual plan take into account the needs of each of these aspects of ministry development?

Is the calendar balanced? Do we have too much going on during certain months and not enough during other months? Momentum requires good, consistent activity flow. But too much going on wears people out and ultimately reduces momentum. Event dates are adjusted to support momentum and in some cases reduced to slow the activity flow. We are ever mindful of the demands made on the family and plan accordingly. In studies done by Stanford University they recognized the Boston area as the fastest-paced city in the United States.[1] We take the opportunity to regulate ministry activity flow so it complements family lifestyles and doesn't compete with it.

Can we afford it? Are we planning too many events that require a lot of investment or cash flow? Our policy is to have the funds available in advance for all the events we plan. All events must pay for themselves—with few exceptions to that rule. Another question: do we need to raise money to cover the expenses for certain events? If so, we try to avoid multiple fundraisers within the same time frame, realizing the hardship that places on families. We consider the cash flow needs for both the church general fund budget as well as the church member's family budget.

Has the ministry been fruitful? Every ministry within the church must be proven worthy to continue into the next year. The regional team and the churches' executive leadership team reviews the effectiveness of each ministry.

The regional team overviews the local church calendar as well as the regional calendar for final adjustment, input, and approval. We learned that if we were going to empower our leaders for ministry we had to involve them and their leaders in the entire process. We also found that when more people were involved, it took much more time to reach a conclusion. Consequently, we had to move our annual planning dates from December to November, and now to October.

It was time well spent, though, when we saw the difference it made throughout the ministry. It was not just putting things on a calendar. It was planning a calendar that was the fulfillment of our vision and purpose. The annual calendar planning sessions provides an overview of the entire ministry and ensures that we are providing adequate care and leadership to the entire flock of God. It also helps to develop a healthy and sustainable pace and flow of ministry activity. Each year we add, delete, or move events and needs arise—we remain flexibly structured.

Having an action plan calendar affords us the opportunity to be proactive regarding future personnel and other ministry needs. As our ministry expanded we trained every staff minister to lead a team. Now some of them are leading and pastoring their own church. And as a result of planning ahead we could determine a plan and process for recruiting and training our future leaders. We haven't hired any outside pastoral ministry staff for years. As a result of planning ahead we see what Dean Radtke calls a "leadership engine"[2] develop. Knowing what we're going to be doing 18 to 36 months from now helps us stay focused on continued leadership development.

Too Much Planning?

Is this too much planning for a Spirit-filled church? At one time in my life as a "Spirit- filled pastor" I would have asked, "How can the Holy Spirit move with everything all planned out like that?" My answer now: the Holy Spirit can move even more when the Holy Spirit leads the leader to lead the leaders. Our activities and events are reflections of what God is speaking to us. If He wants to make a change, we make it. Our plans are subject to change. God made man with a mind to plan knowing that we would need His guidance to adjust our plan.

Proverbs 16:9 (AMP) says: "*A man's mind plans his way, but the Lord directs his steps and makes them sure.*" The Scripture doesn't say not to plan. We must plan and trust that He will direct or redirect our plans.

In planning ahead and delegating to others we free ourselves to spend more time in prayer and study. We also become more focused on leadership development because we have planned far enough ahead that others can now lead and manage the day-to-day ministry. In my attempt to be "Spirit led," I had relinquished my responsibility to be strategic and purpose driven. What good is being "Spirit led" if others aren't empowered to follow me as I follow Christ?

As charismatic Christians we are renowned for trying to do everything that needs to be done all in one church service, and it's all done spontaneously of course. We've also been known to make everything a worship service whether it is a wedding, a home meeting, or a board meeting! You talk about making a truth the truth. I believe we need to move away from being event focused to being more process focused. The great commission is not a command to make worship services. *The great commission is a command to make disciples of all nations.*

At the same time, I am a worshiper; and I could never compromise my deep core value for Spirit-filled praise and worship in my devotional life as well as in corporate worship, prayer services, retreats, and conferences. We have seen significant transformation in our lives after several evenings of worship along with guest ministry. Some sins and weakness are like stains on our soul. Those stains just don't come out without spending time soaking in the presence of the Lord. Worship is irreplaceable in its place. Corporately we continue to take the time to seek the Lord and worship Him in our regular church services and believers' meetings. When it comes to fulfilling our God-called purpose, we must commit action to it and assign time on the calendar when we will do it. It's biblical according to Ecclesiastes: "*To every thing there is a season, and a time to every purpose under Heaven*" (Eccles. 3:1).

People are transformed through a process that includes important events like being born again, water baptism, being filled with the Spirit, becoming a member of a local church, being involved in ministry, and becoming a ministry leader. Some will also move on into full-time ministry. We need a Holy Spirit-inspired plan for that process since that's what God has called us to do. Seasons and times must be planned for His purpose to be fulfilled. In our experience the more we have planned (always subject to change) the more purpose has become fulfilled.

God has put His purpose in our heart and He reveals it to us in installments as we learn to follow Him and continue to grow and mature enough to inherit it completely. He doesn't reveal all of the future work or plans that He has for us, but that's no excuse for us living as though He has no plans for our future.

> *He hath made everything beautiful in His time: also He hath set the world into their heart, so that no man can find out the work that God maketh from the beginning to the end* (Ecclesiastes 3:11).

We are sojourners and shepherd journey takers, not merely educators. God has planted His divine purpose (plan) in our hearts knowing that we will need His help to identify, understand, and fulfill it. Its unfolding discovery and fulfillment has and will continue to bring us great blessing and satisfaction. Only then will we live the life He intended us to live. His plan fits our identity, personality profile, education, background, and family. Life sure is lived the best when it fits us. I'm no longer laboring to live my life by following after another man's plan. We make a connection with the eternal when we connect with and fulfill our true life's plan. I like the Amplified Bible version of the same Scripture in Ecclesiastes:

> *He has made everything beautiful in its time; He also has planted eternity in men's heart and mind* [a divinely implanted sense of a purpose working through the ages which nothing under the sun, but only God, can satisfy], *yet so that man cannot find out what God has done from the beginning to the end* (Ecclesiastes 3:11).

We have had to alter or even cancel our plans on many occasions when the Lord redirected us or revised our vision. In the Book of Acts the Lord redirected Paul or forbade him to go the way he'd planned. Failed plans have often served us well as educational opportunities. I would rather make wrong decisions and change those decisions as opposed to living an unplanned, fearful life of indecision.

LEADERSHIP AND MANAGEMENT

Planning alone, however, won't assure that our purpose is fulfilled. Every successful organization moves down two tracks. One track is leadership. The other track is management. For the benefit of understanding the difference between management and leadership we separate the two tracks in our ministry, though they at times overlap.

I've heard it said that "leadership is doing the right thing" while management is "doing things right." From a leadership point of view, we need to do the right things right for the people we minister to today. Leadership dictates that we retool to reach today's people. I've attended churches that are doing very excellent ministry. Everything is well planned and executed. The only problem—they are not in touch with the present-day culture. They speak the language of a century ago, operate at about the same level of technologically, and dress about the same era as well.

Someone needs to invite them to join the 21st century! They have been playing reruns for too long. They need to make some serious leadership adjustments. I recently attended a charismatic church service that was a flashback to the late '70s or early '80s. There was no meaningful song selection order during the worship time; and most of the songs were old or unknown. People were doing their own thing during the service—some were drinking coffee and snacking while others were twirling streamers. Some stood, others sat. Some sang, others milled around. This is one aspect that I didn't like in the

'70s and I had even less tolerance for it now. This particular church service lacked both good management and leadership!

On the other hand, I know some very cutting edge contemporary churches that are culturally relevant and spiritually in tune. The problem: they are "sloppy agape"! A few examples: the words on their multimedia presentations are misspelled; there are no greeters for visitors; the facilities are usually cluttered; the service never starts on time and always runs later than expected. I visited a church like that when on vacation in Arizona. Shortly after arriving, I asked several people where the pastor was. They had to point him out to me because he was dressed very casually. I was told that he was a great speaker and always had a good message—but I had a hard time getting past how messy the messenger was.

Great ministry management makes a difference in terms of people being able to give and receive ministry. Doing things well tells God how important He is to us. It also tells others how important they are. The early pioneers of the Methodist church, John and Charles Wesley, had a core value of honoring people. They required every minister in their denomination to make a vow never to be late for an appointment. They started their Spirit-filled, miracle, worship services on time without fail.

In my opinion we dishonor people when we don't value their time. Everything we do in ministry must be worthy of the great sacrifice that our Lord Jesus Christ made for people. We should never allow anything to be showcased on our ministry platform that we wouldn't want multiplied a thousand times. Everything we do for God and His people should communicate their great value in Christ.

Low-quality ministry service is the product of low-quality self-worth. The people we minister to in the church know that subconsciously. When we give them low-class, substandard ministry they know that we think less of them. How does that affect them? They will usually live out what they believe to be true about themselves. How can we preach to folks about living a godly, faith-filled, superior lifestyle while at the same time our ministry presentation and environment is so substandard that it makes them feel unimportant and worthless?

I know some Christians who feel very uncomfortable when they visit churches that have a high-quality facility and ministry presentation. They think it's too "uppity" for them. They complain that the people there are just too fancy and dressed up. I think these people would be more comfortable if the churches they visited would accommodate their low self-esteem. They sure are going to have a hard time in Heaven. Heaven is beautiful and affluent because it's the place where Jesus Christ has gone to prepare for us. God shows His value for us in the quality of life that He gave for us and the quality of life He desires for us now and for eternity. Prosperity is an identity issue for Christians. It comes with who we are. We can only be uncomfortable with being prosperous if we don't know who (whose) we are.

I can remember being invited to someone's home once (I wish it only happened once) for dinner. When my wife and I got there the place was a disaster. Their house was unclean, their children were messy and unruly, and they hadn't even begun making the meal. I think they expected us to help them clean the house, take care of the children, and help make the dinner! It made me feel like I wasn't very important to them. There had been no real preparation for our dinner visit. *Value of service should reflect the value of those being served.* Good ministry management has a very powerful identity impact! When you treat people like they're valuable and important, they tend to live up to that expectation.

I bought a second home in Florida and planned to base my traveling ministry operations from there. Since I wasn't there all the time, I decided to have the property management company rent it to Disney-going vacationers. The company representative told me, to my surprise, said that the better a vacation rental home is decorated and maintained, the better the people who rented it would treat it.

I believe the same is true in ministry—better quality ministry management attracts better quality leaders and church members. Quality ministry makes people feel valued and in turn makes them act valuable. They want to live up to how highly we've valued them. Quality music ministry draws quality musicians and vocalists. Quality drama presentations draw quality actors. There's no greater deterrent to recruiting new volunteers and leaders than poor ministry management. Substandard sloppy agape ministry is only appealing to those who haven't discovered their great value in Christ and as a result believe that it's all they are worthy of.

Sometimes we get too familiar with each other in the church and as a result we lower our ministry standards. We need to remember that we didn't die for each other. We don't belong to each other. We belong to Jesus Christ. *He* set the standard for our value by the price that *He* paid for us! He gave His life for us. Excellence in ministry confirms the worthiness of His sacrifice. It's life giving in its impact on those we serve. Excellence in ministry is how we communicate and demonstrate to each other that we're highly blessed and favored. We are affirming the value of who we are in Him and in His Church. Each quality act of ministry service affirms the faith of its recipients and compels them to live at higher standards and levels. According to what is written in the Book of Romans, when we do our sacrificial best in ministry for God we are offering Him an acceptable sacrifice of worship. (See Romans 12:1.)

After we have employed good team leadership in seeking God's direction and purpose and have determined a contemporary, relevant plan of action, we need to move on to team management.

ENDNOTES

1. Levine, Robert V. (1999). The Pace of Life in 31 Countries. *Journal of Cross-Cultural Psychology*. 30 (2): 178-205.

2. Radtke, D. (Speaker) (year unknown). *Buiding a Leadership Engine* [Audio Recording]. Publisher unknown.

CHAPTER 11

TEAM MANAGEMENT

After the regional and local church ministry action plans have been completed and approved, the next step is to develop good ministry management plans. The advantages of planning ahead are numerous. Throughout this chapter I use our Churches in the Lead model for successful management examples—these principles can be adapted to a variety of ministry environments.

TEAM MANAGEMENT BENEFITS

An example of good regional management is special presentations. Inspiring and dynamic ministry guests are invited to come and minister in all of our churches during one trip. That way we can share the costs for advertising, travel, and lodging—saving our ministry time and money. As a result we can afford memorable guests as well as have them visit more often.

We also share offices with our churches that are within a half hour of each other's sanctuary locations. Right now our Woburn, Haverhill, and Manchester churches share their offices and administrative staff and space.

In our Eliot, Maine, church office, we share a financial administrator that handles the finances and recordkeeping for all of our churches. The Eliot church office provides all the administrative support for their church as well as all of the regional administrative support. We team up and share staff, facilities, and equipment for maximum mutual benefit. We do our multimedia productions together and two of our churches share a youth pastor.

We are also able to offer better health insurance as a larger ministry than we could as individual churches. I've already mentioned the benefits of teaming up for world missions.

Each church also contributes toward the cost of supporting me (their apostolic leader). They benefit from my ongoing leadership development and apostolic oversight.

PROJECT PLANNING

From the regional calendar of events, we develop a Churches in the Lead Annual Project Planning Agenda (APPA). On the annual project planning agenda we list every individually planned regional event, the event date, the project planner due date, and require the person who is responsible (team leader) to submit a completed Project Planner. The annual project planning agenda lists individual events or projects chronologically and separates each of them by quarter for the year. Color-coding is used to mark events that are regional.

Project planning works the same way in each of our local churches. Each church includes regional projects on their local church APPA if their church is hosting a regional event. Each church also has a Project Manager who holds each staff member accountable for managing his or her projects. The local church project managers (one of the staff members on the pastor's team) collect project planners each quarter and monitor them. They give monthly updates about the projects at the local church staff meetings.

Having an annual project planning agenda and a project manager who monitors each event gives the leadership team not only the "right things" but also ensures that "things are done right." The list provides accountability for every event scheduled throughout the year.

Each local church and regional ministry's individual Project Planners are due at least 90 days ahead of the event date. Some events are due 180 days (or longer) before the event depending on the size of the event. The lead time makes it easier for all leaders involved to keep track of the project schedule and updates.

As regional executive leader, I assign check-up dates for future events and projects to discuss at future Churches in the Lead staff meetings so I can monitor progress right up to the event date. (Now I have a staff person who does most of this administrative oversight for me.) As a new quarter approaches, we are certain that we're on time and on target for all upcoming events.

Each quarter the executive leadership team also receives completed budgets, check requests, and bulletin announcement forms with each project planner. Every person on staff regionally and locally has a chronological list of projects that they are responsible for annually. This helps them stay focused on being prepared and updated on their upcoming projects and events.

We have also developed a project planning manual that explains how to plan all the different projects and events. The project planning manual is an effective tool and model to train leaders to plan and execute ministry projects and events. Templates for forms and paperwork are on our web site, available for our leaders to print out for their use.

As each event date draws closer, each team leader for that event gives an update or asks for input from the executive leadership team. Calendar changes can be made up to 90 days before the event takes place. The only calendar change that can be made less than 90 before the event is to move the event to another quarter or cancel it. After the Project Planners have been turned in (90-180 days prior) and approved by the team, they are monitored to ensure effective execution right on through to the event date.

Each local church pastor, with the help of the Project Manager, oversees their staff ministry team's projects and events the same way locally as I oversee our team's projects and events with each of them regionally.

This type of management track empowers local and regional pastors and leaders to lead their teams to manage themselves. After all of our teams have been empowered, we (the pastors and apostolic leader) are freed up to oversee things and focus mainly on the development and multiplication of our down-line leaders. Weekly staff meetings are no longer going over the same old, same old.

This type of management style also empowers the administrative staff to develop their own plans and schedules to support the ministry. They are empowered through proactive planning to do their jobs without the constant interruptions characteristic of short-term, reactive situations.

Because Project Planners are turned in three months before the event, office managers can plan their priorities and set their agendas accordingly. Bulletin and multimedia announcements can be produced and the work flow can be planned in advance. Volunteers can be recruited and scheduled to help make flyers and posters, and assist with mailing and phone calls to ensure successful events. Supplies (ink, paper, pens, materials, stamps, etc.) can be ordered and received. Facility and equipment use and maintenance can be scheduled. Maintenance personnel can also be scheduled (recruited first, in some cases)—in some (charismatic church) circles, this would qualify as an authentic miracle!

PROJECT PLANNING BENEFITS

Project planning allows leaders to determine ahead of time the leaders and volunteers they will need to recruit and prepare or train to serve and lead their events for the year.

Helps ministry needs can be defined and schedules determined for ushers and greeters. Opening and closing the facility is also scheduled quarterly. When we have a written plan and schedule for facility use we know who was using the building if we found it unlocked. This also helps improve security measures.

The music ministry can schedule singers, instrumentalists, choir specials, and audio and video for regular services and special events. They can also plan to learn new songs and make arrangements for any drama presentations. Leadership training and development or curriculum can be planned for the quarter as well, based on the Project Planner.

The children's ministry can schedule volunteers for regular and special events. They know how many new people they will need to recruit as leaders and volunteers having already planned ahead for the regular and special events.

Every quarter each ministry turns in a copy of their schedules, check requests, budgets, announcement forms, and Project Planners. Management works best when it is done with team oversight and accountability. The team leader is ultimately responsible for getting everyone's paperwork in on time. If someone doesn't turn in their paperwork, some peer pressure is applied.

Every team member knows that it takes all of us doing our part to achieve our core value of excellence in ministry. Poor management ultimately leads to losing people from our church or possibly losing them eternally. That reality sheds an entirely different light on the importance of team ministry management. When we lose a teenager from the youth ministry we may also lose their mom from the music ministry and maybe their dad from the helps ministry. Everyone is affected each time a person on our team fails to perform in their area of ministry.

As a team we share the responsibility for accountability and correction. When we correct each other it greatly improves the chances that the correction will be received positively. Correction is for our benefit. Godly and healthy correction is actually an investment made by those who love us and who want to improve our behavior in order to improve the quality of our life as well as those around us. That's the way our heavenly Father corrects us according to apostle Paul who wrote about correction in the Book of Hebrews.

> *For whom the Lord loves He chastens, And scourges every son whom He receives. If you endure chastening, God deals with you as with sons; for what son is there whom a father does not chasten? But if you are without chastening, of which all have become partakers, then you are illegitimate and not sons. Furthermore, we have had human fathers who corrected us, and we paid them respect. Shall we not much more readily be in subjection to the Father of spirits and live? For they indeed for a few days chastened us as seemed best to them, but He for our profit, that we may be partakers of His holiness* (Hebrews 12:6-10 NKJV).

Correction done the right way adds value to our lives and has a positive effect on our self-image. Inappropriate behavior or performance is bad for us and hurts others as well. Our staff has learned to appreciate when one of our peers points out something that hurts us or others. Peer correction is one of the greatest benefits of team management.

When we started holding each other accountable as team members our performance improved dramatically and greatly benefited the whole team as well as the church. It can get very uncomfortable at times in staff meetings when everyone around the table asks, "Why don't you have your paperwork in on time? Did the dog eat it?" It wasn't until we moved to team accountability that we were able to get everyone to turn in their paperwork and get things done on time.

I was teaching about team accountability in a large church in Colorado. They were just starting to transition from top-down leadership accountability to team leadership accountability. One of the members of their pastoral staff team went on vacation leaving their department of ministry totally dysfunctional and unprepared. Several of the other pastoral team members noticed the problem and fixed it before he returned. They also unruffled some feathers of those who had been left to catch all the balls dropped by the vacationing team member.

In the process of fixing the problems, they uncovered a lot of other things that needed improvement in that ministry department. The other team members were very supportive of the vacationing staff member in his absence in communicating with his leaders and volunteers who were voicing their ongoing frustrations and problems.

When the pastoral staff member returned from vacation, two of the ministry staff team members confronted him about what had happened while he was gone. They were very loving and humble in their approach and even offered their help to get things turned around in his ministry department. They were following through with what they had all agreed to do—hold each other accountable for their behaviors and performances.

The corrected staff member who had invited his peers to hold him accountable in theory didn't respond very well when they actually held him accountable. He responded initially saying, "I don't have to answer to you. I only answer to the senior pastor." Becoming offended, he demanded a meeting with the senior pastor and the whole team thinking that he would convince everyone that he had been mistreated. Well, it didn't quite go that way. They all agreed that his performance was the issue and the other team members were just trying to help him.

He was even more offended when they tried to reason with him; and he resigned. This was the senior pastor's first experience with team (peer) accountability and he saw the fruit of it. For the first time in his many years in ministry he wasn't the "bad guy" when someone on his ministry staff didn't work out. He was now, for the first time, in a position to minister to the exiting staff minister who wasn't offended with him personally.

After the resignation, unlike before, the pastor didn't have to try to strategize with his wife about what they would tell the church. Everything happened right out in the open and every ministry team leader was in agreement as to what had actually happened. The pastor didn't have to defend himself (unlike previous confrontation experiences) to the other staff members and leaders as to why brother so-and-so quit. No one questioned whether the pastor was inappropriate or had mistreated the staff member.

The whole team had participated in the correction. They had handled it appropriately and as a result, the corrected staff member was given a great opportunity to improve his ministry. He could have greatly improved his leadership skills and ministry craft but instead he received their correction as a personal insult.

The senior pastor called me, excited. "Pastor Ron, this team thing is really working for us. It's moving us to a whole new level." He said that situations like what had just happened with the failed staff member would have set them back in many ways. Behind the scenes, political battles would be waging between the constituencies of those for the departed one and those for the pastor. Over time these kinds of confrontations have an eroding affect on the congregation's trust toward their pastor. As a result, the pastor becomes feared and even eyed with suspicion in subtle, if not direct, ways. Pastors are human too and they can mishandle conflicts and confrontations on occasion—but the enemy is very good at making the pastor think it is entirely his fault.

ETERNAL OFFENSES

With team leadership and management we've learned how to avoid all of the usual negatives inherent with top-down leadership conflicts that ultimately result in ministry staff changes.

It gives me great pleasure to help pastors and leaders avoid some of the heartaches that I've experienced in the past as a top-down leader. Just when we reached our highest level of church attendance, we would be set back again and again by the departure of an offended leader or staff member. The enemy knows the best ways to interrupt the momentum of a growing church. Another thing that grieved me was that the whole congregation would be disappointed every time this scenario repeated itself. I felt as though it was my fault that they were so disappointed.

Jesus said that in the last days people would be offended which would cause conflict, then the deceivers would cause love to fade between the people and many will depart from the faith.

> *And then many will be offended, will betray one another, and will hate one another. Then many false prophets will rise up and deceive many. And because lawlessness will abound, the love of many will grow cold* (Matthew 24:10-12 NKJV).

I will never forget the lesson I learned about the importance of confrontation as a new Christian. At the time, I was
working at a shoe store in Sanford, Maine. Everyday at break
time I walked down the street to buy an ice cream cone. Each
day the Holy Spirit prompted me to share the gospel with the
middle-aged man who owned the ice cream stand, but I didn't
want to take the chance of offending him or making him think
less of me. On one particular day the Lord was really convict-
ing me to talk to him about salvation. I was the only one there
and it was the perfect opportunity, but I chickened out and
didn't say anything. I felt bad that I had given in to my fear but
knew that God would understand why I didn't obey Him. That
night the man had a heart attack and died!

I realized right then just how important it was to stop
being so self-centered. People miss Heaven because selfish
Christians care more about others' approval than we care
about their salvation. It broke my heart at the time and
opened my eyes to see just how serious the consequences are
when we cower from fear of conflict and confrontation.

Team management and leadership have raised our ministry to a new level of maturity, community, and performance.
From a management perspective every team—from the
regional team to the local church pastoral team and down-line
ministry teams in the churches—holds each other accountable
for their behaviors and performances. It results in greater
management because everyone turns in their ministry plans,
calendar of events, project planners, budgets, schedules, and
paperwork on time. This empowers every team to provide the
support and oversight needed for everyone to succeed.

STANDING MEETINGS

Regional Churches in the Lead Team Meetings are held
monthly with the pastors and me to manage and lead our

region. Part of the agenda is reporting and monitoring upcoming regional events. In this all-day meeting, leadership development is our main focus. Management is secondary.

Quarterly management meetings are held in each church with all the core leaders. At the quarterly management meetings the previous quarter is evaluated and the next quarter planned.

Staff meetings for the pastoral staff ministry teams follow-up the core leader quarterly management meetings. Each pastoral ministry team reviews the quarterly plans and makes any final decisions on the upcoming quarterly projects and events.

Monthly pastoral staff ministry team meetings focus entirely on managing and monitoring upcoming projects and events.

Weekly or biweekly pastoral staff ministry team meetings focus on the leadership development of the team members. One of the agenda items may report on upcoming projects or events should they need closer monitoring.

These structures, processes, and systems are set in place to assure quality and excellence in management and at the same time free up the pastors and his or her team members to focus mainly on leadership growth and multiplication. If you don't have good management systems, processes, and structures, you will be constantly distracted with what has to be done or what has to be done right.

I find that many organizations—if not most—are over-managed because they are under-led. Leaders have to spend too much time on management issues because they haven't taught their leaders how to lead others to better manage themselves. They end up *building large bureaucracies instead of large leaders* who can actually do what they said they would do. That's why we include the leaders at every level in the goal setting and planning process. They tell us what needs to be done, and when it needs to be done, and we simply hold them and their teams to it.

I'm amazed at just how far some top-level leaders will go to try to make their subordinates do something that they don't want to do. They keep writing new policies and laying out new hoops for subordinates to jump through. Some top-down leaders judge the staff and make them follow, but they don't take the responsibility to lead them. Jesus said that we're not supposed to judge each other's motives.

Judge not, and you shall not be judged, Condemn not, and you will not be condemned. Forgive, and you will be forgiven. Give and it will be given to you: good measure, pressed down, shaken together, and running over will be put into your bosom. For with the same measure that you use, it will be measured back to you (Luke 6:37-38 NKJV).

From this Scripture we can see that how we lead others will determine for the most part how they will follow us and perhaps how others will follow them. If we don't like what we see happening or harvesting in our church leadership, perhaps we need to take a closer look at what we're seeding into them. Have we as leaders focused too much on making people *do* things? At the same time are we unjustly judging them because they don't want to do those things? Or do we need to focus more on envisioning and including them by taking the time to influence them so they will want do the things that need done?

And what if they don't want to do what needs to be done or want to do what we're doing? I'd say that we should help them find another church or job that has what they want and is more compatible with them. But what I see more often than not, is that the entire ministry becomes over managed because of a few who don't buy in. Too often ministries set new policies and hire new people so the people who don't want to comply will be appeased. I've decided now that if people aren't with us and have no desire to buy into our team-up leadership and management style, they need to move on before too much disruption takes place.

CHAPTER 12

LEADERSHIP DEVELOPMENT

As a pastor, I used to prepare for staff meetings by putting together a "to do" list. Staff meeting agendas centered on what needed to get done and who was going to do it. Very little time and attention was devoted to developing the individual team members. In a top-down structured organization, whether it's a business or a church, there's not much need for leadership development since there is really only one leader— the top person! Everyone else is a worker. The leader gets the credit and reaps the rewards for everything that is accomplished and they get paid to help us. If they don't do what their paid to do, then they are fired or pressured to improve or resign.

In my top-down leadership structure there was no opportunity or plan in my ministry for others to someday have what I had and do what I did. Without realizing it, when I led the church as a top-down leader, I was setting myself up to reap a harvest of top-down leaders just like me who used to worked for me and sooner or later wanted to have what I had. They wanted to be the boss, receive the credit, and reap the rewards of their own ministries. When you have a "me only" ministry you are destined to get a "me only" ministry harvest. Apostle Paul reminded the Galatians about the consequences and rewards of reaping what you sow.

Be not deceived; God is not mocked: for whatsoever a man soweth that shall he also reap. For he that soweth to his flesh shall of the flesh reap corruption; but he that soweth to the Spirit shall of the Spirit reap life everlasting. And let us not be weary in well doing: for in due season we shall reap, if we faint not. As we have therefore opportunity, let us do good unto all men, especially unto them who are of the household of faith (Galatians 6:7-10).

You'll notice he says "*we reap*" in due season if we faint not. Before I became a team player I had a "me only" plan. In turn, I was producing "me only" leaders who wanted to be the top person calling the shots, making the decisions, and reaping the rewards. Some left the church and started their own—usually taking some of your congregation with them. These situations caused the congregation to choose sides and in some cases the pastor isolated himself in an effort to avoid the criticisms of those who left or those who were affected by those who left.

This creates a dysfunctional environment that can last until the pastor moves on or retires. This situation leaves the church vulnerable should the pastor's vacancy happen suddenly or tragically. If there is no succession plan in place and no one is trained to lead the church after the pastor is gone, the church is likely to decline in attendance or in the worse case scenario, it completely dissolves.

A "WE PLAN"

A "we plan" provides leadership development for all potential leaders. Offering them the opportunity to do what the pastor is doing prepares them for multiplying the church—not dividing the church. Realizing the need to raise up leaders within the church through developing a team-up leadership style assures a successful and healthy long-term ministry.

Ultimately, the "we plan" means that the senior pastor must transition into the apostolic and become the regional leader who leads a team of pastors who have been raised up within the apostolic leader's ministry. The apostolic leader reproduces pastors and then he or she continues to lead the multiple church ministries regionally.

There is no greater leadership influence and accountability than relationships. God does everything through relationships. Leadership happens best through relationships—not ruler-ship. There is a place for ruling and governing but that's not how we operate primarily. We value the role of relationships in leadership and its effect on accountability and cohesion.

For example, there is no need for concern that the pastors in each of the planted churches will wonder out of the ministry pattern and do their own thing. First of all the apostolic leader and other pastors have an ongoing relationship with each other. The apostolic leader is on a continual spiritual journey of leadership growth and development with his team of pastors. He or she pastors the pastors on their team. Apostolic leaders are spiritual fathers (regardless of gender) to the pastors they serve. Each pastor also has peer relationships with the other pastors on their regional apostolic team. They are being mentored not only for their present pastoral ministry but also for potential future apostolic ministry.

This "we plan" does not require the "original top-down pastor" to sever relationships with the churches that they have planted or adopted. He or she simply leads now in a different way and gets compensated for all the churches that they lead. We have found that we have to reward productivity and reproduction if we want more of it. The more churches that the apostolic leader leads, the more he or she is rewarded.

ACCOUNTABILITY

There is *one non-profit corporate structure* under which all of our churches operate. This corporation owns all assets for the churches. We also have a board of directors who are apostolic or prophetic in gifting who provide big-picture accountability and oversight to our ministry.

In Churches in the Lead, apostolic structures, processes, and systems are set in place in each church and region to ensure accountability in the following ways:

The Team-up Model brings accountability to all leaders and defines how people are led. Ministries within the church cannot adopt a top-down or consensus-driven structure. The team model defines how leadership happens.

Healthy Team Function brings accountability to team and leadership relational health. Every leader knows when dysfunctions appear and they are held accountable to make appropriate adjustments, build, and maintain healthy relationships with those they serve with.

Team Covenant brings accountability to individual leadership responsibility and corporate team commitment. Everyone knows what is expected of them in terms of how they operate as a team member.

Pattern of Ministry brings accountability to cohesion and conformity to our house DNA. Our ministry is defined so no one can make us something different. All of our leaders understand that all ministry activities must be in keeping with our house Pattern of Ministry.

Vision and Goals bring accountability to all leaders when planning ahead. Each church has the same vision although the goals for carrying them out may vary. On the vision and goals are the fingerprints of each pastor on the apostolic team.

The Annual Calendar of Events brings accountability to action. Every church has a complete and comprehensive action plan that is reflected in their annual calendar. By planning ahead we can provide oversight and leadership to each church's actions and activities to guarantee its integrity and cohesion to the ministry of the house of Churches in the Lead. We can tell by their annual plan if they are in sync with our identity and have a good harvest strategy.

The Administrative Calendar brings managerial accountability and includes project and event planning and oversight. Each event and project on the annual calendar is scheduled and placed on the Annual Project Planner List. During quarterly management meetings, individual Project Planners are completed and turned in for review and revision to assure successful project and event execution. The administrative calendar provides details from which leaders can determine if excellence in administrative management is being accomplished.

Annual Budget brings financial accountability to the annual plan and day-to-day operations. Each church has an annual budget that empowers the pastor and lead team financially. Each church plans its own budget subject to the approval of the apostolic leader and board of directors. The pastor has complete financial authority within the boundaries of his or her annual budget in the local church. Each executive team member on the pastor's team has financial authority within the boundaries of their specific annual budget.

The Churches in the Lead treasurer oversees expenditures in each church and coordinates them for effective cash flow. The pastor, apostolic leader, and board of directors must approve requests for large expenditures of non-budgeted items or over-budget items. Financial operations are centralized through a Churches in the Lead office. The pastor in each local church is not burdened with financial day-to-day operations. Bills are paid as the budget dictates. Non-budgeted or over-budgeted items are paid after approvals have been given. Check requests are made by the pastors in each church and sent out by the Churches in the Lead financial office.

Individual leadership development brings stewardship of leadership accountability. The apostolic leader coaches and mentors the pastors on their regional team. The pastors meet weekly with each of their executive team leaders. They also meet together as a team in weekly or bimonthly staff meetings. Pastors lead their teams as life coaches and mentors. Each executive team member meets regularly with their secondary teams and they follow the same pattern through every team on every level in the church. When leaders reproduce leaders, we experience *addition* growth. When teams reproduce teams, we experience *multiplication* growth!

Team multiplication brings accountability to team reproduction. Each team member's goal is to raise up a secondary team or down-line team of new leaders and lead them together as a secondary team leader. They continue to serve as a team member on a higher-level team. Every team leader coaches and mentors their individual team members with the goal of making each one a leader of their own team. Primary teams hold each other accountable for developing the leaders in each of their secondary teams.

Each accountability structure keeps the ministry healthy and productive. In a team environment, a pastor or a staff member can't just do their own thing. We decide together where we're going as a regional team and then hold each other accountable to stay the course. We can, however, change the course as a team, within the boundaries of our Churches in the Lead apostolic structures and sound doctrine. If other churches want to join our ministry, they have to be willing to adopt our vision, goals, and apostolic structures as their own. We help them assimilate into a new way of thinking because we consider ourselves to be one ministry made up of many churches and, in the near future, many regions.

INDIVIDUAL LEADERSHIP DEVELOPMENT

Individual leadership development is the key to effective team ministry. That's because we're no stronger than our weakest link. At Churches in the Lead, we have a process of leadership development that begins with those entering leadership as small group assistants. We ask that they serve under a small group leader where they can get to know us and grow spiritually. They will then begin the journey of discipleship and leadership development. We use *five levels of leadership* as a guide to develop new and existing leaders. As we get to know the new leaders we help them identify their strengths or gifts as well as any of their specific relational dysfunctions, character flaws, or weaknesses. Then we suggest the courses, books, small groups, or training events that will help them progress first as a person and then as a potential leader.

The new assistant small group leader is mentored and led by their leader who is being led and mentored by an overseer (team leader of small group leaders). The overseer who leads a team of small group leaders also serves as a team member in a higher-level team. From the top down, the leadership flow structure looks like this: Pastor – Team Leader – Small Group Team Leader (overseer) – Small Group Leader – Assistant Small Group Leader.

We evaluate our leaders using the five levels of leadership development:

- Level 1 – Fellowship
- Level 2 – Relationship
- Level 3 – Discipleship

- Level 4 – Leadership
- Level 5 – Craftsmanship

An assistant small group leader begins at Level 3. This person has already been in fellowship with the small group leader and has built a relationship with him or her. The potential leader has asked the small group leader to be a mentor and speak into his or her life. This is where the new leader begins their leadership journey.

At the same time, the small group leader has already been and continues to be discipled and mentored by the overseer leader, who is at least at Level 4 as a leader of leaders. When the overseer develops a down-line of six leaders of leaders he or she moves to Level 5 as a craftsmanship leader.

The following resources are used in our leadership development program. These are only guidelines and suggested resources for leadership development as opposed to set curriculums that don't always fit every individual leader. We also use this resource list as a menu for leaders to choose from when they are looking for options or choices for facilitating their small groups.

LEADERSHIP DEVELOPMENT RESOURCES (BY LEVELS)

Level 1: Fellowship

Fast Start to Christian Living – Richard Booker

The Purpose-driven Life – Rick Warren

His Needs, Her Needs – Willard F. Harley

The Strong-willed Child – James C. Dobson

Bad Girls of the Bible and What We Can Learn From Them – Liz Curtis Higgs

Alpha Courses

Level 2: Relationship

Anger is a Choice – Tim F. LaHaye

Bait of Satan – John Bevere

Battlefield of the Mind – Joyce Meyer

Cleansing Streams – Cleansing Streams Ministry

Growing Strong in God's Family (The New 2:7 Series) – Navigators

He Chose the Nails – Max Lucado

Healing for the Angry Heart (CD Series) – Lisa Bevere

Be Angry (But Don't Blow it) – Lisa Bevere

Me and My Big Mouth – Joyce Meyer

Codependent No More – Melody Beattie

An Ordinary Day with Jesus – John Ortberg and Ruth Haley Barton

Spirit-Controlled Temperament – Tim F. LaHaye

The Purpose-driven Life – Rick Warren

The Search for Significance – Robert S. McGee

What's So Amazing About Grace – Philip Yancey

Twelve Steps to Happiness – Joe Klaas, et.al.

Be a People Person – John C. Maxwell

Winning Ways – Dick Lyles

Intimacy: 100-Day Guide to Lasting Relationships – Douglas Weiss

His Needs, Her Needs – Willard Harley

Homebuilder Series – Family Life

How to Bring Your Children to Christ – Andrew Murray

How to Pray for Your Children – Quin Sherrer and Ruthann Garlock

The Art of Opportunity Parenting – Bill Sanders

The Strong-willed Child – James C. Dobson

Velocity – Blue Fish TV

With Christ in the School of Prayer – Andrew Murray

Bad Girls of the Bible – Liz Curtis Higgs

The Friendships of Women – Dee Brestin

Train Up a Mom – Vollie Sanders

The Seven Seasons of a Man's Life – Patrick M. Morley

Living the High Life – Richard Atherton Bridgeford

The Man in the Mirror – Patrick Morley

Putting Away Childish Things – David A. Seamands

Redeeming the Past – David A. Seamands

I Kissed Dating Goodbye – Joshua Harris

Healing for Damaged Emotions – David A. Seamands

God's Way of Handling Your Money – Crown Ministries

Love Is a Choice – Robert Hemfelt, Frank Minirth, Paul Meier

Boundaries Face to Face: How To Have That Difficult Conversation You've Been Avoiding – Henry Cloud and John Townsend

Wild at Heart – John Eldredge

The Company You Keep – David C. Bentall

Level 3: Discipleship

Anger is a Choice – Tim F. LaHaye

Bait of Satan – John Bevere

Battlefield of the Mind – Joyce Meyer

Breaking Intimidation – John Bevere

Cleansing Streams – Cleansing Streams Ministries

Drawing Near – John Bevere

Financial Guide for Couples (and other books) – Larry Burkett

God's Way of Handling Your Money – Crown Ministries

Growing Strong in God's Family (The New 2:7 Series) – Navigators

He Chose the Nails – Max Lucado

Healing for Damaged Emotions – David A. Seamands

Healing for the Angry Hear (CD Series) – Lisa Bevere

If You Want to Walk On Water, You've Got to Get Out of the Boat – John Ortberg

Intentional Choices – Serendipity

Love Is a Choice – Robert Hemfelt, Frank Minirth, Paul Meier

Making Small Groups Work – Henry Cloud and John Townsend

Me and My Big Mouth – Joyce Meyer

Codependent No More – Melody Beattie

And Ordinary Day with Jesus – John Ortberg

Putting Away Childish Things – David A. Seamands

Redeeming the Past – David A. Seamands

Spirit-Controlled Temperament – Tim LaHaye

The On-Purpose Person – Kevin W. McCarthy

The Power of Spiritual Alignment – Frank Damazio

The Search for Significance – Dr. Robert McGee

Under Cover – John Bevere

What's So Amazing About Grace – Philip Yancey

Bible Studies for a Firm Foundation – Bob and Rose Weiner

Twelve Steps to Happiness – Joe Klaas, et.al.

Ordering Your Private World – Gordon MacDonald

Celebration of Discipline – Richard J. Foster

Be a People Person – John C. Maxwell

Boundaries Face to Face – Henry Cloud and John Townsend

Developing the Leader Within You – John C. Maxwell

Leadership: Biblically Speaking – David Cottrell

The One Minute Manager – Kenneth Blanchard

Thinking For a Change – John C. Maxwell

Winning Ways – Dick Lyles

Your Road Map for Success – John C. Maxwell

Evicting Demonic Intruders – Noel and Phyl Gibson

Gap Standing and Hedge Building – Frank Damazio (tape series)

How to Cast Out Demons – Doris M. Wagner

Intercessory Prayer – Dutch Sheets

Maximizing Your Warfare Potential – Frank Damazio (tape series)

Possessing the Gates of the Enemy – Cindy Jacobs

Prayer Shield – C. Peter Wagner

The School of Prayer – John Brook

They Shall Expel Demons – Derek Prince

Intimacy: A 100-Day Guide to Lasting Relationships – Douglas Weiss

Homebuilders Series – Family Life

How to Pray for Your Children – Quin Sherrer and Ruthann Garlock

The Art of Opportunity Parenting – Bill Sanders

The Strong-willed Child – James C. Dobson

Velocity – Blue Fish TV

I Kissed Dating Goodbye – Joshua Harris

With Christ in the School of Prayer – Andrew Murray

No-Miss Lessons for PreTeens – Group Publications

Smart Choices for Kids – Group Publications

Audience of One – Jeremy Sinnott

Exploring Worship – Bob Sorge and Judson Cornwall

In His Face – Bob Sorge

Extravagant Worship – Darlene Zschech

God's Armor Bearer – Terry Nance

Living an Anointed Life – Kim Wetteland

The Ministry of Helps Handbook – Buddy Bell

Beyond Love – Douglas Weiss

Life Lessons: Books of Ruth & Esther – Max Lucado

Every Woman's Battle – Shannon Ethridge and Stephen Arterburn

Intimate Issues – Linda Dillow & Lorraine Pintus

The Friendships of Women – Dee Brestin

Every Man's Battle – Stephen Arterburn, et. al.

Steps to Freedom – Douglas Weiss

Sex, Men and God – Douglas Weiss

The Seven Seasons of a Man's Life – Patrick M. Morley

Living the High Life – Richard Atherton Bridgeford

The Man in the Mirror – Patrick Morley

Wild at Heart – John Eldredge

The Company You Keep – David C. Bentall

Level 4: Leadership

Intentional Choices, Life Connections – Serendipity

Making Small Groups Work – Henry Cloud and John Townsend

Dog Training, Fly Fishing, and Sharing Christ in the 21st Century – Ted Haggard

Spirit-Controlled Temperament – Tim F. LaHaye

Under Cover – John Bevere

The 17 Essential Qualities of a Team Player – John C. Maxwell

Becoming a Person of Influence – John C. Maxwell and Jim Dornan

Courageous Leadership – Bill Hybels

Failing Forward – John C. Maxwell

Jesus, CEO – Laurie Beth Jones

Jesus, Entrepreneur – Laurie Beth Jones

Death by Meeting – Patrick M. Lencioni

Developing the Leader Within You – John C. Maxwell

Developing the Leaders Around You – John C. Maxwell

Leadership: Biblically Speaking – David Cottrell

The 21 Indispensable Qualities of a Leader – John C. Maxwell

The 21 Irrefutable Laws of Leadership – John C. Maxwell and Zig Ziglar

Today Matters – John C. Maxwell

The Five Dysfunctions of a Team – Patrick M. Lencioni

The Four Obsessions of an Extraordinary Executive – Patrick M. Lencioni

The Five Temptations of a CEO – Patrick M. Lencioni

The Man Who Listens to Horses – Monty Roberts

The One Minute Manager – Kenneth Blanchard

The One Minute Manager Meets the Monkey – Kenneth Blanchard, et. al.

Thinking for a Change – John C. Maxwell

Your Road Map for Success – John C. Maxwell

Multiplication – Tommy Barnett

Evicting Demonic Intruders – Noel and Phyl Gibson

Gap Standing and Hedge Building – Frank Damazio (tape series)

How To Cast Out Demons – Doris Wagner

Intercessory Prayer – Dutch Sheets

Maximizing Your Warfare Potential – Frank Damazio (tape series)

Possessing the Gates of the Enemy – Cindy Jacobs

Prayer Shield – C. Peter Wagner

The School of Prayer: An Introduction to the Divine Office for All Christians – John Brook

They Shall Expel Demons – Derek Prince

With Christ in the School of Prayer – Andrew Murray

Children's Ministry Leadership – Jim Wideman

Leadership Essentials – Craig Jutila

Audience of One – Jeremy Sinnott

Exploring Worship – Bob Sorge and Judson Cornwall

In His Face – Bob Sorge

Extravagant Worship – Darlene Zschech

God's Armor Bearer – Terry Nance

Living the Anointed Life – Kim Wetteland

The Ministry of Helps Handbook – Buddy Bell

The Purpose-driven Church – Rick Warren

Why Not Women – Loren Cunningham and David Joel Hamilton

Beyond Love – Douglas Weiss

Sex, Men and God – Douglas Weiss

Ordering Your Private World – Gordon MacDonald

Celebration of Discipline – Richard J. Foster

The Heart of a Leader – Ken Blanchard

On Becoming a Leader – Warren G. Bennis

Level 5: Craftsmanship

Courageous Leadership – Bill Hybels

Death by Meeting – Patrick M. Lencioni

Developing the Leaders Around You – John C. Maxwell

The Four Obsessions of an Extraordinary Executive – Patrick M. Lencioni

The Five Temptations of a CEO – Patrick M. Lencioni

Silos, Politics and Turf Wars – Patrick M. Lencioni

Multiplication – Tommy Barnette

The Purpose-driven Church – Rick Warren

Why Not Women – Loren Cunningham and David Joel Hamilton

Failing Forward – John Maxwell

Jesus, CEO – Lauri Beth Jones

Jesus, Entrepreneur – Lauri Beth Jones

With Christ in the School of Prayer – Andrew Murray

God's Armor Bearer – Terry Nance

Making Small Groups Work – Henry Cloud and John Townsend

The 7 Habits of Highly Effective People – Stephen R. Covey

The 8th Habit – Stephen R. Covey

Get Better or Get Beaten! – Robert Slater

Quick Team-Building Activities for Busy Managers – Brian Cole Miller

Leading Change – John P. Kotter

Built To Last – Jim Collins and Jerry I. Porras

Good to Great – Jim Collins

The Heart of a Leader – Ken Blanchard

High Five – Ken Blanchard and Sheldon Bowles

Leadership by the Book – Ken Blanchard, Bill Hybels, and Phil Hodges

Gung Ho! Turn On the People in Any Organization – Ken Blanchard, Sheldon Bowles

Raving Fans – Ken Blanchard, Sheldon Bowles

Who Moved My Cheese? – Spencer Johnson and Ken Blanchard

The Big Book of Team Building Games – John Newstrom & Edward Scannell

Make It So: Leadership Lessons From Star Trek – Wess Roberts and Bill Ross

Maximum Leadership 2000 – Charles M. Farkas, Philippe De Backer, Allen Sheppard

Stop Setting Goals (If You Would Rather Solve Problems) – Bobb Biehl

The Leaders of the Future – Frances Hesselbein, Marshall Goldsmith, and Richard Beckhard

Fish! A Remarkable Way to Boost Morale and Improve Results – Stephen C. Lundin, Harry Paul, and John Christensen

You will notice that some books or small group curriculums are listed in more than one level. That's because they can be effectively used in each of those levels. Sometimes leadership needs surface at different levels. As we grow and lead others to grow, we constantly add books and small group resources to the various levels.

EVENTS AND ACTIVITIES

We plan events for the year that guarantee each of our individual leaders, as well as those they lead, to have the opportunity to keep growing and developing. Events are planned to harvest new converts, recruit volunteers, and develop leadership by level.

Before we started defining the process of leadership growth, we noticed growth gaps in our leaders' progress. Without this defined process, it was also difficult to train others to mentor and coach their leaders. Now we plan small group activities that meet the upcoming and current needs of our small group leaders and attendees.

The following list of events is grouped by levels which helps us overview our leadership and discipleship process for balance and continuation. By planning events ahead for the year by Levels 1-5 and by planning small groups for the quarter, we are more strategic about the programs we offer.

Level 1-2: Fellowship and Relationship Events

Mother's Day – free gift and honor given to mothers

Father's Day – free gift and honor given to fathers

Christmas and Easter Dramas and Musicals

Easter Egg Hunt

Illustrated Sermons

Vacation Bible School

Benevolent Outreaches—nursing homes, jails, prisons

Guest Speakers—secular appeal or testimonial appeal

Halloween Fall Festival or Trunk-Or-Treat (a Halloween alternative)

MOPS – Mothers of Preschoolers

Water Baptisms, Baby Dedications

Men's and Women's Breakfasts

Family Events—picnics, movie nights, etc.

Sporting Events—campouts, archery, target shooting, hunter safety, motorcycling, etc.

Youth Events—rallies, lock-ins, paint ball, bowling, skiing, concerts, etc.

Children Events—apple picking, sledding, beach days, etc.

Adult Events—Valentine dinner, Christmas party, progressive dinners, etc.

Father-Son Day, Daddy-Daughter Day, Mother-Daughter Day, Mother-Son Day

Church Clean-up Days

Communion Services

Candlelight Service
Angel Tree Gifts
Guest Receptions
Level 3: Discipleship Events
Freedom Day—healing and deliverance
Guest Speakers—Marriage, Prayer, Singles
Retreats—men, women, youth, and marriage
Church Membership Seminar
Level 4: Leadership Events
Ushers and Greeter Training
Small Group Leader Orientation and Training
Music Ministry Training
Communication Seminar
Prophetic Seminars and Schools
Missions Conference and Trips
Multimedia Training
Audio Training
Children Ministry Leaders Training
Regional Conferences
Small Group Rally Weeks
Level 5: Craftsmanship Events
Core Leader Meetings
Quarterly Management Meetings
Pastor's Appreciation
Sacraments and Ceremonies Training
Annual Staff Planning Days
Staff Off-site Team Development Events
Regional Leadership Training Events
Executive Team Meetings

It's up to the team and individual leaders to recommend what each of their leaders might need to expedite their growth and development as Christians and leaders. Some training events are required for higher level leaders and staff members.

The apostolic leader and team overview the annual calendar of each church to see if their plan for events and small groups is comprehensive and meets all the needs in the following areas:

Community Outreach

Perspective Members

Current Members

Leaders

Staff Members

Regional Leaders

Using the five levels to focus our planning has helped us develop a healthy and balanced ministry. We also ask each other if we have planned too much or not enough. We review past calendar quarters and consider making adjustments that would more effectively meet our community, congregation, and leadership needs.

After we have planned the calendar, screened it by levels, and adjusted it for activity flow, we have completed the process for the year. We still have the option, though, of making calendar and event adjustments quarterly and monthly if necessary. After the calendar has been set, we focus our attention on leadership growth and team multiplication.

MULTIPLYING LEADERS

We found that if we didn't plan ahead we spent too much time managing upcoming events. We would reshuffle things every week to accommodate the event and deplete the time we needed to train and multiply our leaders and teams. Staff and leadership meetings were focused on short-term events rather than long-term leadership development.

Now there are grease boards in our offices where we diagram our leadership flow charts. The pastor is already a Level 5 leader and his or her goal is to bring every leader on their staff team up to a Level 5 leader. Each leader on the pastor's team is evaluated by their leadership level. The pastor has the final say about which level each leader is in.

In turn, each staff member evaluates each of their secondary team members the same way the pastor did. They follow the level evaluation throughout all of the down-line teams. Staff meetings and leadership team meetings focus on the level of their leaders and what they need to bring them up to the next level.

I have worked with some churches using this process that have added more than 120 new leaders in just one year! After the pastor and those on his or her team catch the vision for growing the church through leadership multiplication, it really takes off. The goal is team multiplication, not just leadership multiplication.

The traditional church growth model is set up for adding people (consumers) to the church. We have found that the team leadership multiplication model moved us from addition (of consumers) to multiplication of people (leaders) to the church. We are no longer just feeding people through our ministry; we are now helping every lay person discover their God-given ministries. Our main focus is to help them reach their community through their ministries, by developing them as Christians and leaders. Our ministry functions to disciple them and help them start and develop their own ministry.

Advancement in leadership and ministry takes place as we help others advance in their leadership and ministries. To date I have reproduced myself six times as a pastor. In addition to leading our churches, I am working with other pastors as well to help them reproduce themselves as pastors and become apostolic leaders.

I believe the new move of God will be a multiplication movement. The apostolic and prophetic gifting will be the keys to transitioning the church into that new movement. Divine strategies and designs are just now being revealed to the church in preparation for the next apostolic and prophetic multiplication move of God. That's what happened in the Book of Acts; and that's what is going to happen again!

I see thousands of pastors in America transitioning into the apostolic ministry in this new move of God. Ministries will then be multiplied through these leaders as they hasten the second coming of Christ. The entire planet could be converted in a short time with the exponential multiplication of leaders and converts. One of the biggest obstacles to pastors catching this apostolic vision is our obsession with becoming megachurch pastors.

PARTNERSHIPS

I'm not against megachurches; we need everyone we have to bring in the harvest. We need the megachurches as well as the multiplication of apostolic (regional groups of churches) networks. There are many areas around the country that are not populated enough to build megachurches but they could flourish with multiple churches that unite for regional impact and world harvest. I work with several megachurch pastors who have a vision for world harvest and church planting. They have the resources to multiply their leaders and ministries even more. We're not competing with them, we're partnering with them.

I believe that some of our individual churches in the Churches in the Lead regional network will grow to become megachurches as well. Pastors in less populated areas who lead multisite churches could potentially become megachurch pastors who lead apostolically as well. Megachurch pastors could also have the potential to lead networks of churches that they have planted and/or adopted.

It all starts, however, at the grassroots level of leadership development and multiplication. The team structure provides the right kind of environment for that to happen. Without a team structure there is more of a tendency for leaders to become self-protective, competitive, and isolated.

God is once again breathing a fresh breath upon us that we, like the first group of 12 disciples, can only catch as a team. He always sent them out in teams, trained them in teams, and grew them up in teams. God cares about who we are becoming as well as what we are accomplishing. He chose a team to accomplish His ministry and to multiply it.

There is nothing new under the sun—we are following in His footsteps.

Perhaps you are not sold on multiplication ministry? Believe me—it is a real and repetitive biblical harvest principle.

CHAPTER 13

TEAM MINISTRY MULTIPLICATION

Biblically speaking we are to be more than just "fruitful." We are to "be fruitful and multiply." Why is it so important that we be Christ-like? Because whatever we are like is reproduced and multiplied. Not just what we do, but who we are as well. We are made to be fruitful and multiply.

> *And God said, Let us make man in our image, after our like-ness: and let them have dominion over the fish of the sea, and over the fowl of the air, and over the cattle, and over all the earth, and over every creeping thing that creepeth upon the earth. So God created man in his own image, in the image of God created He him; male and female created He them. And God blessed them, and God said unto them, **Be fruitful, and multiply**, and replenish the earth, and subdue it; and have dominion over the fish of the sea, and over the fowl of the air, and over every living thing that moveth upon the earth* (Genesis 1:26-28).

Man is by physical design tremendously fruitful! One healthy male produces 500,000 human seeds a day. Think about that! There is something of great value in each of our lives in addition to the physical seed that waits to be discovered and multiplied.

In the life of every man and every woman is a divine deposit of greatness that awaits our recognition, discovery, and multiplication. Some people have multiple deposits of talents, gifting, and anointing. But the impact of those deposits is not felt completely until the deposits are multiplied. What are you doing with what God has given to you? In the parable of the talents we see how God feels about wasted talent.

For the kingdom of Heaven is like a man traveling to a far country, who called his own servants and delivered his goods to them. And to one he gave five talents, to another two, and to another one, to each according to his own ability; and immediately he went on a journey. Then he who had received the five talents went and traded with them, and made another five talents. And likewise he who had received two gained two more also. But he who had received one went and dug in the ground, and hid his lord's money. After a long time the lord of those servants came and settled accounts with them.

So he who had received five talents came and brought five other talents, saying, "Lord, you delivered to me five talents; look, I have gained five more talents besides them." His lord said to him, "Well done, good and faithful servant; you were faithful over a few things, I will make you ruler over many things. Enter into the joy of your lord." He also who had received two talents came and said, "Lord, you delivered to me two talents; look, I have gained two more talents besides them." His lord said to him, "Well done, good and faithful servant; you have been faithful over a few things, I will make you ruler over many things. Enter into the joy of your lord."

Then he who had received the one talent came and said, "Lord, I knew you to be a hard man, reaping where you have not sown, and gathering where you have not scattered seed. And I was afraid, and went and hid your talent in the ground. Look, there you have what is yours."

*But his lord answered and said to him, **"You wicked and lazy servant**, you knew that I reap where I have not sown, and gather where I have not scattered seed. So you ought to have deposited my money with the bankers, and at my coming I would have received back my own with interest." So take the talent from him, and give it to him who has ten talents.*

*For to everyone who has, more will be given, and he will have abundance; but from him who does not have, even what he has will be taken away. **And cast the unprofitable servant into the outer darkness. There will be weeping and gnashing of teeth** (Matthew 25:14-30 NKJV).*

How does God respond to wasted talent? Talent is a gift from God and He will hold us accountable for what we do with it. Talent's greatest impact is realized when we multiply it through others.

ADAM AND EVE AND NOAH

God's plan for humankind has always been a plan of multiplication blessing. Starting with Adam and Eve, multiplication was man's original mission. After the flood Noah and his family multiplied the population.

And God blessed Noah and his sons, and said unto them, Be fruitful, and multiply, and replenish the earth. And you, be ye fruitful, and multiply: bring forth abundantly in the earth, and multiply therein (Genesis 9:1,7).

ABRAHAM AND ISAAC AND JACOB

God gave Abraham a multiplication covenant as well.

Neither shall thy name any more be called Abram, but thy name shall be Abraham; for a father of many nations have I made thee. And I will make thee exceeding fruitful, and I will make nations of thee, and kings shall come out of thee. And

181

I will establish my covenant between me and thee and thy seed after thee in their generations for an everlasting covenant, to be a God unto thee, and to thy seed after thee. And I will give unto thee, and to thy seed after thee, the land wherein thou art a stranger, all the land of Canaan, for an everlasting possession; and I will be their God (Genesis 17:5-8).

Generational blessing is a multiplication blessing because when we have children and they have children, we multiply.

God continues the multiplication blessing with Abraham's son, Isaac.

*Sojourn in this land, and I will be with thee, and will bless thee; for unto thee and unto thy seed, I will give all these countries, and I will perform the oath which I sware unto Abraham thy father; And I will make thy seed to **multiply** as the stars of heaven, and will give unto thy seed all these countries; and in thy seed shall all the nations of the earth be blessed* (Genesis 26:3-4).

God again blesses Isaac's son, Jacob, with the multiplication blessing.

*And Isaac called Jacob, and blessed him, and charged him, and said unto him, Thou shalt not take a wife of the daughters of Canaan. Arise, go to Padanaram, to the house of Bethuel thy mother's father; and take thee a wife from thence of the daughters of Laban thy mother's brother. And God Almighty bless thee, and make thee fruitful, and **multiply thee**, that thou mayest be a multitude of people; And give thee the blessing of Abraham, to thee, and to thy seed with thee; that thou mayest inherit the land wherein thou art a stranger, which God gave unto Abraham* (Genesis 28:1-4).

Notice that Jacob had to have the right wife. Jacob also had to have the right kind of life. The story is all too familiar. Jacob had to go on a spiritual journey and experience a spiri-

TEAM MINISTRY MULTIPLICATION

tual transformation of character. God was careful to mold Jacob's character and life in such a way that when it was multiplied the spiritual DNA remained intact. Doesn't that sound familiar? That's why it can take so long for God to release us into ministry.

We don't have a clue how much we need to be transformed and changed. I long for the day when the church in the United States once again values Christ-likeness.

Jacob births a nation that inherits the multiplication blessing.

> *And God said unto him, I am God Almighty: be fruitful* [addition] *and **multiply**; a nation and a company of nations shall be of thee, and kings shall come out of thy loins; And the land which I gave Abraham and Isaac, to thee I will give it, and to thy seed after thee will I give the land* (Genesis 35:11-12).

Like Jacob, we aren't ready to experience great multiplication without a great personal transformation. Without great transformation we end up in a great mess. We actually end up reproducing our problems in the lives of others. That's why we have to lead transformation through transformation. Others we lead grow in Christ-likeness and leadership as they follow us in our growth in Christ-likeness and leadership.

I used to feel like the red-headed stepchild (I actually had red hair as a child) that had been left behind. I often wondered why God wasn't blessing me. Now, I'm so glad He didn't multiply me when I thought I was ready. God often lets us have our own way; until we're convinced it's not what we want.

God blessed Israel through multiplication blessing. God does not change throughout the Old Testament. He repeatedly says and does the same thing—be fruitful and multiply.

Jesus Christ spoke of Himself as a seed sown that multiplies until it reaps a global harvest: "*Verily, verily, I say unto you, Except a corn of wheat fall into the ground and die, it abideth alone: but if it die, it bringeth forth much fruit*" (John 12:24).

MULTIPLICATION IS GOD'S PLAN

Multiplication is God's plan for prosperity, posterity, and legacy. When I reproduce myself (in Christ) in ministry, my ministry continues to produce and reproduce reproducers long after I'm gone. That's why my personal Christ-likeness is so important. God loves us enough to perfect and mature us so we can reproduce after our own kind. It's not just ministry work that we reproduce and multiply. We multiply the work God has done in us through others who are our spiritual offspring (leaders).

Others don't have to start in life or ministry where we started; they start where we ended and continue on. Apostolic ministry is foundational. Others build their lives and ministries upon a solid Christ-like foundation.

In the charismatic church today, leaders are starting out where we did 30 years ago. I don't want them to start where I did. If they do, then I believe that I've lived and ministered in vain. With that, I leave no generational life legacy. People in business, education, art, technology, and practically every human endeavor, all pass on what they have and what they've learned—all except the charismatic church.

Our independent, entrepreneurial leadership style has to transition to team multiplication before it's too late. Already I've noticed that many of my pastor friends' ministries have ended or have been redirected from its original purpose and vision, shortly after the pastor passed on.

God's plan for the Church has always been and will continue to be multiplication. The early church had to transition into multiplication ministry. In the beginning of the Book of Acts, the Lord added to the Church. *"Praising God, and having favor with all the people. And the Lord **added to the church** daily such as should be saved"* (Acts 2:47).

The first five chapters in the Book of Acts tell about additional (and in the case of Ananias and Sapphira, subtraction) of church growth. Why was the Lord so seemingly hard on Ananias and Sapphira? Perhaps they threatened to compromise the DNA for those who would come after them. In being dishonest about their commitment they would have had an even more negative impact when their lives were multiplied in others.

There's a greater vulnerability when we transition from addition ministry into multiplication ministry. Foundational leaders have a greater accountability because they will set the bar for those to come after. Mathematics change from addition and subtraction to multiplication in the sixth chapter of the Book of Acts.

> *And in those days, when the number of the disciples was **multiplied**, there arose a murmuring of the Grecians against the Hebrews, because their widows were neglected in the daily ministration* (Acts 6:1).

There it is—the multiplication ministry. Although they were *multiplying disciples*, they were stopped dead in their tracks by having to perform the duties of pastoral care to the widows. The daily administration of the widows was being neglected until they made a leadership structural change. The ministry in terms of ownership belonged to the apostles only up until that point.

The same thing is stopping us today. Feeding people has replaced the agenda of reproducing disciples (leadership) which includes feeding them. At this point the early church leaders had to make a decision: Are we going to be the feeders or the multiplying leaders?

The church model in most churches in the United States is much like a restaurant. People are fed but they don't necessarily follow Christ completely in their lifestyle. Our codependent culture accuses us of neglecting the care of people if that's not our primary mission. In turn, many churches today are developing a feed-only ministry program. Consequently, people don't journey toward transformation, they consume. The early church made the right choice. They transitioned from addition ministry to multiplication ministry. *"And the Word of God increased; and the number of the disciples **multiplied** in Jerusalem greatly; and a great company of the priests were obedient to the faith"* (Acts 6:7).

The disciples multiplied and then we see that the churches multiplied.

> *Then had **the churches** rest throughout all Judaea and Galilee and Samaria, and were edified; and walking in the fear of the Lord, and in the comfort of the Holy Ghost, were **multiplied*** (Acts 9:31).

It's time to change from addition to multiplication in our churches in the United States so we can experience God's multiplied blessing. The great commission is God's revealed plan to every believer and to every church.

> *Go ye therefore and teach all nations, baptizing them in the name of the Father, and of the Son, and of the Holy Ghost: Teaching them to observe all things whatsoever I have commanded you: and lo, I am with you always, even unto the end of the world. Amen* (Matthew 28:19-20).

The great commission is the multiplication of disciples into all the nations of the world. We have to change our mission of making meals to making disciples. That leads the way to transitioning from addition ministry to multiplication ministry. We do multiplication ministry the way Jesus Christ did it, through small group ministry multiplication.

Things get done in the ministry when there is ownership by those involved. For example: If I asked the average church member, "Are the church vehicles clean?" Most would not know. But if I asked, "Is your vehicle clean?" they would respond right away. Why do you know the condition of your vehicle, but not the condition of the church vehicle? The answer: ownership.

Ownership changes with a transition from addition ministry to multiplication ministry as follows:

In *addition* ministry, I help:

- the pastor or a staff minister with his or her ministry.
- serve the pastor or staff minister.
- support the pastor and staff ministry.
- pray for the pastor and his or her ministry.
- the pastor succeed.

In *multiplication* ministry, the pastor or staff minister helps:

- me with my ministry.
- me recruit others to serve in my ministry.
- by helping me build, develop, and support my ministry.
- by praying for my ministry and teaching me how to pray for others in my ministry.
- me succeed in life and ministry.

In *addition* ministry, anything pastors do is out of the goodness of their heart. However, they have a limited amount of time to give, to pray, and serve in your ministry. No wonder the widows were being neglected! There's no ownership in that. Until we change from *addition* (I'm helping pastor) ministry to *multiplication* (the pastor's helping me) ministry, we'll continue to be plagued with the following dysfunctions:

- Lack of volunteers.
- Negative attitudes from church members
  "I'm being taken advantage of" by the ministry staff.
  Accusatory and guilty feelings (I'm not committed if I don't do this or volunteer for that...)
- 80 percent of the work is done by 20 percent of the people.
- 80 percent of money received is given by 20 percent of the people.
- An us (church members) and them (church staff) attitude.

Multiplication ministry will not work unless you have real buy in with ownership. Until the lay leadership in the church owns ministry, there will be a dearth in volunteerism and workers.

Jesus Christ supernaturally ministered and led His leaders, modeling the multiplication ministry. He multiplied the loaves and fishes on several occasions by handing out the bread and fish through the hands of the disciples to the multitudes. In one of the events there were 12 baskets leftover. That would have been enough for one basket for each disciple or leader.

Multiplication ministry, when applied right, leaves us with more than enough to meet all our needs. On the other occasion of bread and fish multiplication, there were seven baskets remaining. Seven is the number of completion. Multiplication ministry assures that things will get done or completed and there will be more than enough remaining for the ministers to meet their own needs. In other words, ministry won't exhaust all of the personal resources and energy of the ministers when they learn to work through others.

JESUS, OUR MODEL

I believe Jesus was mentoring His disciples in multiplication and the miraculous. I also believe that people and resources will be supernaturally supplied to the leaders who are willing to reproduce themselves in others who in turn reproduce reproducers. Jesus said the Father God was like a husbandmen or vineyard owner. His job is to make sure the vineyard (us) produces much fruit.

> *I am the true vine, and My Father is the vinedresser. Every branch in Me that does not bear fruit He takes away; and every branch that bears fruit He prunes, that it may bear more fruit* (John 15:1-2 NKJV).

The Lord is clear about this—He is looking for fruitful reproduction. "*Herein is my Father glorified, that ye bear **much fruit**; so shall ye be my disciples*" (John 15:8).

God is glorified only when we're fruitful! He's at work in those and does a work in those who bear much fruit. The best method of stewardship for people and resources is to multiply them.

In *addition* ministry, all the people come to me. In *multiplication* ministry, I go to the people through others under my leadership. Jesus went to all the people—first Himself, then through the apostles and their followers, and so it goes.

CHURCHES IN THE LEAD MINISTRY MULTIPLICATION

In our ministry, the pastor leads a team of six leaders or ministry staff who in turn each lead a ministry team of six leaders in the church. Those who follow him or her follow the pastor's lifestyle and leadership.

The lifestyle and leadership is then modeled and followed by those who are led by the ministry staff. The pastor limits their leadership access to no more than six leaders. Those leaders under the pastor in turn lead a team of no more than six leaders.

Why do we limit ourselves to no more than six direct report leaders? We have found that more than six leaders are too many people to engage in effective team ministry. It's important to remember that every team leader also serves as a team member on a higher level team, making a total of 12 when you add the teams together. The team leader models team building with his or her team with the goal of transitioning every team member into team leaders.

For too long churches depended solely on the pastor. In that top-down structure the pastor influences a large group (typically Sunday mornings) to a very small degree. That's why there's so little character difference in the life of the average Christian. Pastors need to have more influence on each individual person. *The typical pastor spiritually influences everyone at about the depth of a communion wafer.*

The objective of the multiplication ministry is to go back to the Jesus model by developing a greater depth of leadership influence with the team around the pastor who in turn develop a greater depth of leadership influence with the people they lead. Teams under these leaders multiply until those in the pews are positively influenced and on board with the house core values, vision, mission, and lifestyle. The pastor and leaders have more time to be with the Lord and with their families, which sets the right lifestyle example for everyone in the church.

Team multiplication not only reproduces character and values but it is also the best way to bring numeric growth to the church. Every new leader is trained to lead a small group. They have to reach new people and recruit them from within and without the church. One of their goals is to raise up an assistant leader from within their group to begin their leadership reproduction process.

We're no longer just adding more people to the pastoral care list for him to take care of. Every new leader provides about 75 percent of the pastoral care to the people who attend their group. Their up-line of leadership and pastoral staff members provide the remaining 25 percent. The pastor provides the pastoral care for the individual pastoral staff team members. The apostolic leader provides the pastoral care for the six pastors on his or her regional apostolic team.

CHAPTER 14

REGIONAL APOSTOLIC AND PROPHETIC TEAMS

After transitioning to a team model, the number of ministries within our church multiplied. We not only multiplied our ministries but we also transitioned from a one church ministry to a multiple church ministry which made us a regional ministry. As a leader, I no longer pastor a church but I pastor a region and look to multiply the regions by reproducing other apostolic team leaders. We team up to plant and adopt new churches and expand into new regions. I'm also currently working with other apostolically gifted pastors who are transitioning into multi-church and multiregional ministry.

I have seen the importance of working together with prophetically gifted leaders in this entire process. Prophet Ed Traut has been used by the Lord to give us insight into God's direction for our ministry. Ed also works with many of the same apostolic leaders that I work with. God uses the prophetic ministry to help our leaders see God's future for them.

Our leaders have been greatly impacted and ignited spiritually when a prophet has spoken very accurately about their journey with God and His desires for the future ministry. When leaders hear God's word for them, they are ready to go! Unfortunately, until we had a team-up ministry of multiplication in place, they had nowhere to go. When a prophetic ministry came to our church, people would get excited but quickly fizzled out—diminishing the effectiveness of the prophetic ministry. People begin to doubt the prophetic when they don't see results. The end result was just a bunch of hoopla and over time people lost interest in and questioned the validity of the prophetic ministry.

God uses the apostolic ministry to develop the leadership and ministry structures, processes, and systems that help new leaders move into their prophetically recognized ministries. The pattern provides a track for the potential leader to follow right into their God-ordained future. The *prophetic ministry* imparts insight to the believer and the church as to what God is saying to them. The *apostolic ministry* provides oversight to the believer and to the church for the stewardship of leadership structure and development.

As an apostolic leader I can have all the systems, processes, and structures in place for leadership advancement and development. However, if the leaders don't know that God has called them or if they lack the motivation to move into their calling, they will not benefit from or respond to my ministry. In other words, if the prophet makes the baby jump (like Jesus and John the Baptist did in the wombs of their mothers), they still need a place give birth. Leaders may recognize that they have a ministry in seed form, but they need to know that there is somewhere it can be planted and a process begun to bring it to fruition.

The pastor assists those who have received prophetic words by clarifying and validating the prophecy and pastoring them through it. The apostle assists those who have verified a ministry calling recognized by valid prophet ministry, by developing and cultivating them to maturity. Both the apostolic and prophetic ministries need each other and must operate together in order to get maximum results.

Because I had witnessed some questionable prophetic ministries over the years, I wasn't open to having prophetic ministry in our churches. Although I had also seen legitimate prophetic ministries who had prophesied many accurate words to me and others, yet not all their words had come to pass.

I believe this doubt delayed our transition into the apostolic as well as the transition of our leaders into their unseen ministry callings. Something was missing and knew it was the prophetic when we met Ed Traut who shed some light on the subject. His prophetic words to us and our church members came to pass in mass—and in short order. God was confirming that we were finally on the right track.

As I transitioned from pastoring a church and leading several other churches into full-time apostolic ministry, the Holy Spirit began to give me insight into the structures, processes, and systems that we needed to develop in order to better employ and empower our leaders. As we obeyed His directives He moved us to an entirely new level. Leaders and ministries multiplied quickly. My frustration began to dissolve as I understood clearly how God wanted to operate through the team multiplication ministry.

OBSTACLES AND BENEFITS

One of the greatest obstacles in making the transition into apostolic leadership is the idea that pastors becoming apostles have to give up their salary and financial authority in order to make their transition. It's probably the biggest reason why many pastors haven't transitioned into apostolic ministry. The Churches in the Lead (CITL) board of directors and I agreed that I should be paid and authorized as though I was the pastor (now apostle) and Chief Executive Officer (CEO) of the region.

The CITL board of directors consists of (outside) apostolic/prophetic ministers with whom we have had a long-time relationship. They empower me and hold me accountable to give oversight to all of our churches. I'm subject to them, and to the vision of the house and accountability structures of CITL. I have complete operational and financial authority. My ministry salary and expenses are paid by the network and expensed internally to each of the church budgets. We have one ministry—financially, as well as spiritually.

I have executive authority over all CITL staff ministry wide. The pastors have the same executive privilege in each of their churches and are subject to me. Each staff member has the same privilege with their areas of ministry and is subject to their pastor. Each pastor's salary and ministry expenses are dispensed to their church accordingly.

We are one ministry and work together as a team and don't see each church as having complete autonomy. As we multiply new regions, each apostolic leader serves and leads up to six churches. Every pastor has complete availability to their regional apostolic leader. The apostolic leader works together with the pastors to develop a comprehensive vision and action plan for their region. The pastors do the same thing with their team in each local church.

Every pastor has the opportunity to grow into a regional apostolic leader. My mission as a regional leader is to unite, build up, and expand our regions by providing leadership development and pastoral care to every pastor and church. Each pastor's mission is to do the same thing in their local church.

We have regional conferences that include both apostolic and prophetic ministries that provide both insight and oversight to our leaders and future leaders. The prophets make their "babies jump" and the pastors and I help them deliver their babies (ministries) when they come through the apostolic leadership process to full term.

Some of our church members who were with us for years and going nowhere in leadership are now in full-time ministry serving the Lord. The church service with the highest attendance is the one when a prophetic ministry is brought into the house. The apostolic ministries help us bring new and existing leaders to the next level of leadership. Our pastors become excited when the apostolic and prophetic ministries come to their churches and conferences and help them harvest and mature their leaders for the glory of God!

Apostles and prophets are God's servant leaders to the pastors and churches. The five-fold ministry gifts of the apostle or prophet are not superior to the pastor ministry gift. I still think that being a pastor is the highest calling one can have in the Kingdom of God. Jesus is the Great Shepherd not the great apostle. Apostles and prophets are needed in the Church to help the pastors mature and harvest souls for Christ.

Apostles leave their legacies with their spiritual sons and daughters who continue their lifetime pastoral work that would have otherwise ended with them. Apostles are like the grand-pastors (spiritual grandparents) to their churches. I tell our pastors that I don't want them to start where I started almost 30 years ago. I want them to stand on my ministry shoulders and start where I left off. I want them to build on top of what I built.

The pastors are the inheritors of all that I am in Christ and in the ministry. I am their servant and spiritual father who longs to see them reach their greatest heights and accomplishments for the Kingdom of God. I trust and pray that they will exceed me greatly. I'm also called and entrusted by God to provide the spiritual leadership and oversight they need to do the same with their spiritual sons and daughters. We're growing together in our spiritual journey toward Christ-likeness and Kingdom expansion and succession.

WORDS FROM GOD

Together we are praying for God to help us plant and establish, in my lifetime, hundreds of churches. Before moving to Massachusetts from Alabama in 1986, I received a prophetic word that we would have hundreds of churches from Maine to Florida. At the time, I thought that word was more "pathetic" than "prophetic," but have since changed my attitude and opinion.

The prophet that spoke that word over me did not know me. He did not know that I used to pastor the church he was speaking at just a few months earlier. I was sitting in the middle of the congregation when he picked me out. In the 1980s and early '90s I received words from the Lord by Prophet Bill Hammon about the apostolic call of God on my life. He foretold much of what has happened in our ministry since that time.

Another prophet, Claire Meade Huck, also prophesied to me about the apostolic calling upon my life and foretold with great detail what has now become our history. She said that we would have other churches within the region that would all be connected as one ministry. She spoke of the structure of it as being like a wheel with spokes going out of it. She also told me to study the honey bee and how they as a species build and function. We now have a honeycomb-shaped team model with six sides representing six leaders on each team with down-lined or multiplied honey combs.

For years I ignored those prophetic words and just hunkered down and did what I believed God had called me to do. I didn't know how to respond to the prophetic words and direction we had received. I was frustrated and unfulfilled for much of that time until I realized that I had to make a paradigm shift and start moving into the destiny God set for me. In reality I was functioning in apostolic ministry for years—I just called it "multi-sight" ministry. It doesn't really matter the title—it matters that you move into your calling.

TITLES AND ROLES

It does matter, however, what you call yourself if you are going to reproduce yourself in others. The first thing you have to do before you reproduce something is define it.

When I finally transitioned to leading our network of churches I called the local pastors the "resident pastors" and referred to myself as the "senior pastor." As time went by and I was not able to attend each church regularly, that title and role became an issue. When I would speak in one of our churches, I would be introduced as the senior pastor and new people would get confused and say, "Oh, I thought that (the resident pastor) was the senior pastor." There was a disconnect because they had never seen me before or perhaps not regularly. They felt less cared for, thinking that I abandoned them for something more important.

I was reluctant to use the big "A" word, not knowing what newcomers would think about it. I didn't want to use the "bishop" title because it communicated something Roman Catholic in some people's way of thinking here in New England. I also didn't want to reduce the identity of the local church pastors by calling me the pastor and them something less than the pastor. They asked if they could refer to me as the Churches in the Lead apostle. I felt a little uncomfortable with it at first but have learned to adjust to being called an apostle if it helps the congregations better relate to me. I was a little more comfortable with "apostolic leader" at first and now I'm OK with them calling me Apostle Ron here in our own ministry.

When I travel and work with other churches they usually refer to me as Pastor Ron, an apostolic leader. It really doesn't matter as much to me what I'm called as long as I am received and can minister to everyone effectively.

I've had this conversation with other pastors I respect who are very reluctant to call or be called an apostle. They may not even be pastoring a church and functioning completely as an apostolic leader, but they still hesitate being referred to as an apostle. These same ministers had no hesitancy being called pastor when they were pastors. Perhaps our hesitancy will change in the coming years as more and more pastors transition into the apostolic ministry.

THE TIME IS NOW

As the deadline approached for submitting this book for publication, we had just concluded a regional apostolic/ prophetic conference titled "For Such a Time as This." I believe it's more than a coincidence that the conference concluded the same time as my publisher's deadline. I believe that the apostolic and prophetic move of God is a very current, unfolding revelation for the Body of Christ. We have historically made progress and moved forward in ministry before realizing it. All of the sudden we recognize what happened as we look in the rearview mirror.

Once we realize where God is leading us, by acknowledging where He has just taken us, we can plan to make progress—on purpose. The Holy Spirit recently used Prophet Dennis Cramer to help us see even more of the divine tactics for the ever-expanding vision of Churches in the Lead. He confirmed prophetic words spoken by Clair Huck in the '80s, Bill Hammon in the '90s, and Ed Traut in just the last few years. The prophetic words spoken over the last 20 years by these prophetic servants of the Lord have all been cohesive, consistent, and connected. It has truly amazed me how they can say the same things yet reveal new things in the unfolding revelation of God's plan for us and those we love and lead.

We've seen the prophetic gifting increase when we had more than one prophet minister together in our conferences and meetings. They have an amplifying affect on each other. Faith grows in the hearts of those who hear their prophetic words from more than one prophet. Joe Nay had never met Dennis Cramer before they came and ministered separately in each of our churches and prophesied to hundreds of people. They were saying very specific things to individuals on different nights or services, yet they confirmed each other's prophetic words to the same individuals. It was as if they had compared notes—but they didn't, they were sharing words from God.

Hearing God's words for them impacts people in a way that prompts them to action. They want to do something for God when they hear from Him. Leaders with specific tactical directives like a call to serve God in youth ministry or children ministry are ready to be trained and deployed. Others who are called to the nations are ready to pursue missions and perhaps take the next mission trip. Those who hear a prophetic word about an emotional injury that is hindering their lives and ministry are ready to get healed. Others who have not been very committed to God or ministry are now ready to get committed.

God-called prophets help us mobilize and activate our leaders and congregants by helping them to hear a "now word" from God. The apostolic leaders of Churches in the Lead have to agree with the words spoken before people are encouraged to act on them.

We don't have just anybody come and prophesy in our ministry. They have to be proven in their gifting and character. Prophets must be able to preach and teach and prophesy. I believe that a prophet who only prophesies and can't preach and teach is not really a New Testament prophet. I told one young man who only wanted to come and prophesy and receive an offering that he wasn't a prophet—he was a fortune teller. That's not to say that a prophet has to teach every time he or she ministers in one of our churches. But they have to be able to teach and preach and prophesy.

We have also seen God use the prophets to reveal tactics and details that have identified, helped, and brought direction to many of our business people. The gifts of healing and miracles have also manifested in both the prophetic and apostolic ministries. People who couldn't conceive for years have had babies within a year after receiving prophesies. Financial miracles have followed as well. It's no wonder that people attend Holy Spirit-led apostolic/prophetic team ministry services.

The apostolic ministries have helped us to apply wisdom to circumstances in the church as well as with individual Christians and leaders. They teach on leadership and reveal divine strategies for growing our churches as well as our businesses. Some of them have been very successful in business as well as ministry. Leading and managing a successful church has a lot in common with leading a successful business. Many of our business people and marketplace ministers apply our team models and concepts to their businesses. The thing we have in common is people. Leading people is leading people whether in church or in business.

We need to be leaders in all realms and spheres of life. Apostolic leaders often have more in common with entrepreneurial business men and women than they do with anyone else in the church. What do we have in common? We're both divinely gifted to be builders and architects of human structures. We both deal with human resources by divine design and capacity. Business people follow our team-up leadership style to lead their businesses. I'm gifted in leadership development and multiplication. They can apply the same principles at work or in their business. Joseph was anointed with apostolic ability and he saved the entire nation of Israel.

The church of the future will produce and lead market-place apostolic ministers who will have divine revelation and strategies for turning the wealth of the wicked over to the righteous in Christ. They will help us fund the last day's harvest of souls with their apostolic wisdom that brings an explosion of new businesses and business expansions. Business problems will be solved by the anointed wisdom of God by these apostolic leaders who are being raised up both in the church and on the job or at their businesses.

Some apostolic business people in the church have been alienated because we have not recognized their value and have treated them like they weren't spiritual. For the most part, they had to teach a Bible study or sing in the choir to be accepted and appreciated in the church. Unfortunately, they haven't found their place because their area of gifting wasn't one that the church acknowledged—until now.

As an apostolic leader I like to recruit business and professional men and women and show them how to build their practices and businesses through leadership and team building. The world is looking for us just like the Pharaoh was looking for Joseph. He could only find Joseph when he found out what Joseph was gifted by God to do.

Apostles are sent to the church to help develop divine strategies for leadership growth and multiplication. Apostolic leaders are multiplication ministers who catch a revelation that will impact us in a way that brings great increase as well as excellence. They are the systems, structures, and process people who God anoints for the Kingdom's growth in excellence and multiplication. It's the same gifting that empowers the Christians who founded and multiplied Chick-fil-A, McDonald's, JC Penney, Colgate, and hundreds or perhaps thousands who carved out our country's business and financial landscape.

Apostolic leaders bring their anointing to the church to help the church grow and multiply. They also bring people in from the business community and stir them up and catalyze them for business outreach, start-ups, and expansion. These leaders can make a significant difference in the marketplace and in the church. They will get the world's attention with their godly wisdom and savvy insight.

Apostolic and prophetic leaders are sent by God to cast their lines into our churches and catch all of our future leaders and ministers who will bring their future into our present. They will help us recognize our gifts and callings and fulfill our God-given destinies. The apostles will help us set up the leadership structures, processes, and systems that will empower, mobilize, and mature leaders so they can fulfill their call and service to the Lord Jesus Christ.

Retooling the Church has led Churches in the Lead to experience growth in leaders and members. Souls have been saved in each of our churches. Leaders have been challenged and trained. Leaders have been awakened to their God-given gifts, talents, and skills. Pastors are excited about leading their new and newly motivated and inspired leaders and followers through the process of transformation. The leaders are excited because they have the systems and processes in place to help their pastor pull in the nets from this great harvest.

Our prayer is that retooling the Church will become a vision for pastors and ministry leaders in every community, region, and across the nation. The team-up leadership model works—the multiplication ministry works. Reproducing the pattern Jesus set in place will bring His Kingdom on earth as it is in Heaven.

Appendix

Leadership Multiplication Flow Chart

Regional Apostolic Executive Team
(apostolic leader and apostolic board of directors)

Regional Apostolic Team
(1 Apostle and up to 6 Pastors representing each church)

Executive Leadership Team
(pastor and ministry team leaders)

Ministry Teams
(local church ministry leaders)
Music ministry leader plus team of 6,
Children's ministry leader plus team of 6,
Small group ministry leader, etc.

Congregates

Additional copies of this book and other book titles from DESTINY IMAGE are available at your local bookstore.

Call toll-free: 1-800-722-6774.

Send a request for a catalog to:

Destiny Image® Publishers, Inc.
P.O. Box 310
Shippensburg, PA 17257-0310

"Speaking to the Purposes of God for This Generation and for the Generations to Come"

For a complete list of our titles, visit us at www.destinyimage.com